For Bella

Happy Mother's Day

May 1995

Love from

Charles & Nancy

THE PASSING

THE PASSING

PERSPECTIVES OF RURAL AMERICA

paintings by
Jim Harrison

words by
Ferrol Sams

LONGSTREET PRESS

For Helen

—F.S.

To My Dady, "Red" Harrison

—J.H.

Published by
LONGSTREET PRESS, INC.
a subsidiary of Cox Newspapers,
a division of Cox Enterprises, Inc.
2140 Newmarket Parkway
Suite 118
Marietta, Georgia 30067

Printed in the United States of America

2nd printing, 1994

Library of Congress Catalog Card Number: 88-081799

ISBN 0-929264-03-7

This book was printed by Arcata Graphics Kingsport Press, Kingsport, Tennessee. The text was set in Palatino by Typo-Repro Service, Inc., Atlanta, Georgia. Design by Paulette Lambert.

THE PASSING

1907
CROSS THIS BRIDGE AT A WALK
JIM HARRISON

THE BRIDGE

BRIDGES please me well. From Golden Gate to Pont de Neuf to the swinging one across Cloudland Canyon, there is a marvel in traveling from this side to that side without getting wet. Bridges extend roads smoothly over impeding natural barriers. When they span the Nile or the Thames or the Amicolola, they are beautifully monumental, manifestations of the thought and labor of those who went before. They make straight the way and smooth our path. Essential to commerce, they are, therefore, lifelines for cities.

Bridges are worth fighting for and have ever been treasures in the purse of Mars. The Greeks were brave at the Hellespont. So was George Patton at the Rhine. He made good his boast that he would arrive at that river with his pontoons and urinate into it while he awaited the arrival of the Russians. The great bridges of history have nurtured capitals and the cycle of civilization.

But, oh, the little country bridges of my youth. Peaceful and lonely most of the time, they were great vantage points from which to look up or down a mysterious creek as it bubbled along through lush ferns or impenetrable vines. From atop a bridge, one could spot spawning suckers in pools below and thrill to the perfume of the swamp, laced with honeysuckle and wild crab but based in the musk of black mud and rotting logs.

Only slithering lizards or a barefoot boy could cross a country bridge in any semblance of silence. A horse might pull a well-oiled wagon down the sandy road with muffled feet, but once

JIMHARRISON

Drink
Coca-Cola
5¢

the bridge was reached, a crescendo of sound erupted. The horse would tense its neck in lovely arc to roll a suspicious eye at the strange structure with cracks in it that gave glimpse into an unknown world below. Admonished by driver's cluck or slapping rein, the animal would give a great challenging snort and leap upon the bridge with staccato hooves. The ensuing bedlam of rattling planks, iron-rimmed wheels and loose railings would awaken the swamp a half-mile downstream. The kingfisher nesting in the bank beneath the bridge would hurtle true down the course of the creek, its body a semaphore of blue and black and startling white, its cry a dry clatter that punctuated the din. Frogs would croak and plop into the water, and a great blue heron might emit a startled squawk before sailing serenely on kite-thin wing into hiding around the bend.

As quickly as it began, the intrusion would be over, and the swamp would settle once more into secrets of silence that a boy could explore in unhurried delight for hours on end. The span of a bridge is a marvel from above, but life beneath it is a wonder, a richness. I remember hunkering beside my grandfather on the banks of Woolsey Creek at the wash-hole beneath the bridge. It was back in the days when the creek flowed clear and clean. You could see the glint of mica in the little brown gravel that rolled along the bottom where it was swift and shallow, and it was all right to drink the water. That was a long time ago.

The time is gone and so is my grandfather, but I recollect him well. With a sinker but no cork, his bait a bit of chicken neck, he was fishing for eels. After long minutes of being very still and listening to the gurgling rush of the creek and the whisper of breeze-lifted leaves, he snatched a prize from the waters. To me it was a snake, a mean and vicious and terribly active snake. Only my dread of appearing puny before the white-haired authority of my grandfather kept me from fleeing through brambles up to the road, shrieking like the daintiest of little school girls. I was terrified. The creature had a tightly packed row of the sharpest teeth I had ever seen, a baleful red eye that was singling me out as an individual, and the most muscular body in all creation, whipping and writhing in violent convolutions as it tried to explode itself from the hook.

My grandfather pulled a glove on his right hand with his teeth, grasped his trophy behind the head, extracted the hook, and deposited the wriggling beast into a croker sack. Then he set in to teach me. Snakes have scales, eels do not. Eeels are so slick that you have to have a glove to hold one and also to keep them from biting you. That's where we get the saying "slippery as an eel." No man alive has a grip strong enough to hold a big eel without a glove.

Eels, he told me, are the slickest things in the world. Then he paused and added, "Almost." You have to carry a sack when you're eel fishing, I learned, because you can't put them on a stringer, and you have to be sure it's a new sack with nary the slightest hole in it or you'll get home without your eel.

"Of course, you don't scrape an eel like a fish, boy; there's nothing to scrape. You cut its head off and skin it with a pair of pliers, like you do a catfish. Eel eats better than catfish; it's meatier and not as fishy. But, son, you have to eat it while it's hot. If you let eel meat get cold, it turns raw again."

I distinctly remember the awe with which I replied, "Yes, sir." I also remember the evasive tactics I practiced at supper that night. I was not brave enough to run the risk of eating cold eel. My grandfather was a rugged man; he also ate chitlins, mountain oysters and pig feet. He would put sugar on a slice of tomato and carry it to his mouth on the blade of his knife, and he poured coffee into his saucer to drink it, right under the silent glare of my grandmother. When he was a little boy, he had even seen live yankees in uniform. He said "pan of my hand" and "holp" instead of "helped." It was said that when he was twenty he had killed a man. The afternoon I fished for eels beneath the Woolsey Bridge, I realized that my grandfather loved me. My presence there assured it, for he was not one who suffered fools gladly.

I remember the eel. To this day when I smell creek water, I think *raw*. I also feel secure. Bridges please me well.

JIM HARRISON

TOOLS

WAY BACK yonder, a man himself had to fix anything that tore up around the farm. Everybody had his own tools. Times were hard, and I do not remember seeing any saws, hammers or planes that were new. Even the nails were old and rusty, pulled out and straightened and used over and over again. When handles wore out, new ones were whittled from hickory.

There was no electricity anywhere around, and therefore nobody had ever heard of power tools. A handsaw did not whine; it made a rhythmic, snoring sound, slowing as it got nearly through the planks so that the cut would be clean. A brace and bit was enticing to behold, curling its way through a board to leave a hole so smooth and round that the perfection of its symmetry was a wonder. The hand plane produced shavings that twisted upon themselves in marvelous whorls as fluffy as a girl's newly set hair and every bit as fragrant. The bubble in the liquid of a level was mysterious, also invoking wonder.

A man who could patch a broken door, put a new spoke in a wagon wheel, replace a rotted board on the barn, or make brand-new steps for the front porch was a plain ordinary farmer. A farmer with extra skills that he more than likely had learned from his father, one who knew how to lay out a foundation, erect a building and put a roof on and who also had the equipment as well as the knowledge, was respected as a carpenter.

Mr. Tom Stubbs was such a man. He was our neighbor down

the road, and anything Mr. Tom couldn't build didn't need building. He was a farmer first and a carpenter second, but he took equal pride in both occupations. He brought his tools and his second son, who had inherited his carpentry talent, and built a two-story corncrib for us that was admired by all who saw it. The first story was slatted to let air circulate freely through the corn that we stored still in the shuck; the second story was weather-boarded on the outside against the rain, then on the inside was tongue-and-grooved in construction so tight that it could hold unsacked wheat.

The crib was proportioned pleasingly too and belonged right where it stood on the skyline of our farm buildings. With the help of a couple of our field hands to lift heavy timbers, Mr. Tom and his boy built the crib one week when it was too wet to plow. During World War II, my mother undertook to burn the garden off by herself, and the crib caught fire and burned to the ground. Otherwise, it would have stood at least another hundred years.

Mr. Tom was a rawhide whipcord of a man who wore tiny little gold-rimmed glasses and taught all his boys to work as hard as he did. Not a one of them farmed for a living after the war was over. Mr. Tom, as he grew older, walked with his hands clasped behind his back and looked more carefully at the ground. He had a ready laugh for a visiting child, although he never interrupted his work to bestow it.

When I was seven, my grandfather let me ride with him on a two-horse wagonload of ribbon cane down to the Stubbs place. Mr. Tom had a syrup mill, and he and my grandfather spent the day hard at work grinding cane and cooking juice, the best of neighbors. My memories of that experience, however, are overridden by what happened to me for tagging along behind Mr. Tom's youngest son.

Weldon Stubbs was about twelve years older than I. Mr. Tom called him "Boy," but to me he was a grown man, all muscled out and straight-backed. He had the thickest hair I'd ever seen, erupting straight up from his scalp like a heavy crop of ripe wheat and then waving over the top like wheat does when wind blows over it in early June. His laugh was quick, his good humor vast, and I was flattered when he visited the syrup mill for a few minutes and invited me to go along while he checked his traps. I thought him the kindest person in all creation and followed him dauntlessly through brambles and vines for a half-hour under the afternoon sun of a warm November day in the woods on the Stubbs place.

Weldon had set out some steel traps in hidden places, baited with chicken scraps from Miss Minnie's kitchen. He hoped for a fox or, better yet, a mink, animals that he could skin out and sell. The first trap was empty, and we trudged ahead to the second, Weldon talking to me all the way.

He stopped abruptly and raised his hand.

"Ferrol-boy, we got something on this one!"

His voice was a coarse whisper, but the excitement in it was contagious. I moved eagerly to his side.

"Pshaw, it's a durn ole polecat. Caught him by his front foot, and he's tore up the ground all around trying to gnaw it off. If it had caught him across his neck, it would of killed him, and I could have got his hide, but there ain't no way now to save it."

I had never seen a polecat in my seven years. I knew they were bad to suck eggs and eat baby chickens, and they could stink up an old dog so that he would roll in the dirt and slink around the periphery of the yard with his tail between his legs for two days, walleyed and grimacing when other dogs fled and humans scolded. Polecats were varmints, and I rushed forward to see one.

Weldon grabbed me. "Don't you go any closer 'til I shoot him; he'll spray you and you'll stink worse'n cairn. Look at him from here."

What I beheld was a little treasure of an animal, brilliantly striped in black and white, plumed tail raised and waving like a feather, small sharp head held close to the ground by the teeth of the steel trap. Like an actor spotlighted in soliloquy, the polecat dominated the sun-streaked glade. Its left front foot was bloody where, mute, desperate, the beautiful little wild thing was staking its life on mutilation to gain freedom.

Weldon raised his .22.

"Don't shoot," I begged. "He's too pretty. Let's get his leg well and tame him. Or at least turn him loose."

"No way to do that, Ferrol-boy. He'll die if we leave him in that trap, and he'll die if he gnaws out, 'cause he's caught too high on his leg. There's nothing to do but shoot him, and I've got to get him in the head so as he'll die before he can spray."

The tense silence of the ensuing moment was broken by the crack of the .22. The arched back collapsed, the tail drifted to the earth, and I dashed forward for a closer look, disobedient to Weldon's shouts to stop.

As I bent over the bright bundle, one hand outstretched to touch the little body, he gave a final twitch, and I fell to the ground retching.

I remember that I had to follow Weldon back to the syrup mill at some distance; I remember that Mr. Tom was the only one who laughed; I remember that my grandfather made me ride home on the very tail end of the wagon tongue, clucking tired mules to a trot to create a relieving breeze. I remember being staked out at the corn crib and told to come no nearer the house. My strongest memory, however, is that of the subsequent half-hour. My mother handed off a towel, a washrag, clean clothes and a bar of Octagon soap to a grown-up colored man and abandoned me. I followed the kindly man a quarter-mile through the pasture to our creek, where he stripped me, scrubbed me with sand and soap, lathered my hair, submerged me three or four times in the icy water of the hole below the white mud cave-in, and buried my tainted clothes. I learned a lot that day.

I learned a lot from Weldon later, too. Just before World War II, they sent him to Colorado for training for ski patrol; then after Pearl Harbor, they shipped him to the South Pacific. He came home, married, got a job in a cotton mill in Griffin and voted as a Democrat all his life. He and his wife never had any children, but they bought a nice home with some acreage and worked until retirement. Last year I encountered him in Dell's

Drive-In, which was really Jim Hancock's restaurant. He was indignant.

"I've been thinking all these years that we won our war, but now I feel like we lost it. When the folks in this county beat them school bonds yesterday, driving around in their fancy cars and yapping about taxes going up, it was a victory for the Communists."

I waited. Weldon never needs a request for elaboration — he is ever ready with one.

"I went overseas in 1942. I shot at a heap of Japs, and I killed some of them. A heap of them shot at me, but I made it back. I went all over the Pacific, and I saw folks living worse than dogs do in this country. The one thing I learned was that you need two things for Communists to take over. You need poverty, and you need ignorance. I ain't got a youngun to educate myself, but we need to quit being selfish and get together. We need to spend the money to teach all the children in this country. If we don't, they'll grow up ignorant, and we're opening the door for the Communists."

Mr. Tom Stubbs could raise sons as well as he could raise corn cribs. Straight and true and built to last. I hope that his tools are not lost.

JIMHARRISON

10 2
Dr Pepper
4
10 2
Dr Pepper
4
JIM HARRISON

PRIVATE LESSONS

*G*IVEN the almost militant credo of some historical societies that anything old should be preserved, it is surprising that there are so few privies left in the land. The structure was ubiquitous. It might be known as outhouse, closet, toilet,

johnnie, the necessary or the facility. Occasionally an even coarser, more graphic term that incorporated function was used, but on every farm a privy was present. A visit to it was referred to as "a trip down the lane," "I had to step out," "I went out," or, somewhat boastfully, "my daily."

Most privies were sturdily built and perky, upright little structures with slanting shingled roof and neatly overlapped weatherboarding. They stood demurely but assertively at the end of garden lane or winding path, isolated from other buildings and also the water supply but never appearing lonely. Kate Greer said they always had a fig bush planted in front of them, but that was her opinion. Kate lived in town.

The privy was not regarded as status symbol in the same fashion that was afforded flower beds and well-swept yards, but there was still a subtle social distinction to be derived from one. A person with pride of place tolerated no weeds around the privy, kept the newspapers or corn cobs neatly stacked and provided a sack of lime with a tin cup. People of substance and principle had a wooden door on their outhouses; a family that tolerated having only a burlap bag to screen the entrance ran the risk of being regarded as trash. There were accounts of people who had only a board laid across blocks, with sacks stretched around saplings for walls and no roof at all. Those folks were worse than trash; they were designated as sorry.

The solid citizen of acceptable lineage and attitude provided his family with a neat, well-kept edifice, weatherproof and snug. Even the manner in which one evacuated one's alimentary canal contributed to the caste system of the South. It was a highly structured society, and it began at the bottom. So to speak.

The seat inside the privy had two holes. I never saw one with only one hole or one with three. I also never saw an occasion when the two holes were utilized simultaneously, although one could endorse the theory that it was well to be prepared for emergency.

Occasionally a chicken would steal a nest in the corner of the privy. It was an easy way to garner eggs, and it was wise to leave a nest egg so that the old hen would return on a daily basis. It was unsettling to burst into a privy unawares, however, and have a startled, squawking Rhode Island Red erupt past one's head with frantic flapping of wings and flurry of feathers. To a sensitive small child, it could be a constipating experience.

Sometimes an old cat would choose the box of newspapers on the floor of the privy as a home for a new litter. It was a cozy, comfortable feeling to sit and watch baby kittens nurse. Who can forget the faint mewling cries of blind babies groping for the sustenance of a nipple? The tottering stance of defiance and the challenging "fftt, fftt" later on when the kittens' eyes opened and they reacted to an intruder? Who has not witnessed a complacent mama cat roll on her back, secure in the presence of a trusted human, and exhibit her rows of breasts, mounding white through the fur still wet from suckling, her nipples as tiny and as delicately pink as the blossoms on a partridge berry?

Most memories of a privy, however, are not pleasant and may well account for the fact that the majority of them were demolished as soon as more modern accommodation could be provided and a farmer could slap a pump in his well. Cats and chickens were not the only visitors to or residents within such a facility. The black widow, wicked queen of all the spiders, having killed her mate with post-coital dispatch, was fond of building her sticky gray nest in the dry shadows on the underside of the toilet seat. From this citadel she attacked all intrusion with the same vigor as a Mother Superior repelling a panty raid, but with more deadly results. The intruders, because of anatomical variation, were always male, and the sex ratio of black widow victims was consequently greater than ten to one, exclusive of the mate.

Mr. Spurlin Banks, protruding into Lady Macbeth's domain one morning while he relaxed in concentrating constitutional, was stung and envenomed by an unusually large and violent member of the arachnoid matriarchy. Mr. Spurlin was a very modest man. In addition, he had been raised right. There were some things that did not warrant discussion under any circumstances, and the location of his injury was one of them. Privates were so labeled because they were supposed to remain just that; in fact, some rural gentlemen referred to the entire conglomerate as "my privacy." Adhering to current local taboos, therefore, Mr. Spurlin delayed reporting his accident until the poison was circulating unchecked throughout his system and had produced unbearable abdominal pain, sweating and shock.

By the time his wife could send to Redwine's Funeral Home for the ambulance to transport him to Crawford W. Long in Atlanta, Mr. Spurlin was so ill that his hospitalization required a week. His misfortune was the talk of the community, but Mrs. Banks was true to the local mores. Not only did she refrain from divulging the site of his wound; she also with some delicacy neglected to tell what Mr. Spurlin was doing and where he was doing it when he was bitten. All that the folks who lived around Antioch Baptist Church knew was that Mr. Spurlin Banks had damned near died from a black widow spider bite. He had been saved by the doctors in Atlanta and the fervent prayers of the Antioch WMS, apparently with equal effort if not conscious coordination.

Convalescing at home, he received a state visit from Miss Winnie Kincaid. Miss Winnie was a confirmed and militant spinster, unforgettable in both appearance and presence. Her hair was gray, pulled back tightly from her face and fastened in secure bun on the nape of her neck with tortoiseshell hairpins. She spurned makeup of any sort and disdained fluctuations of fashion; her skirts were always two inches above her ankles and modestly full. Her eyebrows were the gray of her hair, unplucked and bushy, sheltering cavernous sockets in untamed overhang. The eyes themselves, however, were her most memorable feature.

There was something wrong with Miss Winnie's eyes. She could see a little, but she had to work to do it. She batted her eyelids so fast that they were in a constant flutter. In addition, she rolled her head perpetually in order to bring the orbs into focus, now tilting her chin to the heavens, now burrowing it into her chest, meanwhile swinging her head from one side to the other and back again.

In complement, she also was possessed of a deep, bugling voice, stentorian, authoritative. Coordinating eyes, head and voice, she could rise to her feet and take over any WMS meeting or church conference. The Kincaids had all been raised not to whine but to do the best they could with what they got, and if Miss Winnie was self-conscious, it never showed.

When she paid her condolence call on Mr. Spurlin Banks, she carried him a half-pint of quincedonia jelly and two purple dahlias, which were all she could spare for a sick neighbor, and him yet a man, and have enough left to cut for Antioch Baptist on Sunday.

She came uncompromisingly to the point of her visit, "Spurlin, I'm glad to hear you are able to be up and take nourishment. Where did the spider bite you?"

Mr. Banks nestled his head a little more firmly into his pillows and crossed his hands on the outside of the counterpane. "About one hundred yards due west of here, Miss Winnie, in the edge of that little old sweetgum thicket."

The eyelids fluttered, the head swung far to the left so that the patient could be impaled in shimmering focus. "Spurlin, I ain't talking about where you yourself was at when it happened. I'm a-talking about where was the spider at when he bit you?"

Mr. Banks had a honeyed tongue and great diplomacy when indicated.

"Miss Winnie, I'm here to tell you I had a close call, and I'm thankful to be here. I heard that all you ladies prayed for me at the church, and I sure appreciate it. You should have seen what all they did for me up there at that Crawford W. Long. They must have been four or five or six doctors waiting on me; seemed like they was one in my room ever time you could turn around. And nurses! You never saw the like of nurses in your life. They come through in coveys and was the sweetest, kindest things you could ask for—"

"Spurlin!" Miss Winnie interjected.

Mr. Banks ignored the interruption, plowing smoothly ahead with his filibuster. "—I mean I really got the attention. Day and night what I mean. Somebody was all time looking in on me. Course, they was charging me eighteen dollars a day on account of I had a private room, and I know that's high as a cat's back, but it was worth it to get my life saved. I still got a couple of bales of cotton under the shed, and they ought to just about cover it. The wife and grandbabies—"

"Spurlin," Miss Winnie expostulated. "What I want to know is—"

"And you wouldn't believe what all they put me through. First couple of days they fed me all the time in my veins. Had one jug running in on this side in this here arm, and another jug on the other side in this arm, and time one would get low they'd hang up another one. And shots! My stars, Miss Winnie, you wouldn't believe the amount of shots and the variety that they can poke into a man when he's in a hospital."

Miss Winnie rose imperiously to her feet. Her eyelids rivaled the rapidity of hummingbird wings, her head rolled in emphatic full circle.

"Spurlin, rest your voice a minute and listen to me. Where did that spider bite you *at*?"

Spurlin Banks raised himself up on both elbows, his leonine head defiant, and flung off all pretense at manners.

"Goddam it, Winnie Kincaid!" he roared. "All I'm gonna tell you is that if that spider had of bit *at* you, he'd have missed you!" He pulled the covers over his head and turned his back.

Miss Winnie Kincaid and Mr. Spurlin Banks did not speak to each other again except on the church grounds, and that very formally, for three or four years.

As soon as electricity was strung to that side of the county, however, each one of them closed in one end of the back porch and slapped a pump in the well.

Their privies vanished shortly thereafter.

It was forty years later before the Historical Society was established in Fayette County.

fresh
up with
7up
JIM HARRISON

CROSSING
ROAD
JIM HARRISON

JIM HARRISON

THE SOCIAL HUB

DEPOTS across rural America were so much of a pattern that one suspected the railroad companies had a common set of plans that they enlarged or revised or shifted around a little to give different communities the important delusion of individuality. They all had the same pitch of roof with wide overhang all around that needed only a little uptilt at the corners to make them look Chinese.

My friend Newton Gaddis, who was twenty years older than I, always said that the depot was the social hub in our town. Folks went up to Atlanta in the morning and returned from Atlanta in late afternoon on the train. People congregated at the depot daily to watch the evening train come in, to see who had been to town that day and with whom, to survey and assess any stranger that alighted, to exchange news when it was available and gossip when it wasn't.

The mail truck was a flatbedded wooden wagon with no side rails. It had an iron tongue and iron wheels, its bed higher than a small boy's head; it was distinguished from the baggage cart by "US GOV'T." lettered in black with gold highlight across its side. It waited on the platform so near the tracks that the heavy canvas mailbags could be swung directly onto it from the mail car when the train stopped.

A man was hired for a pittance to struggle and pull that mail truck two blocks across town to deliver the locked mailbags to the post office. The social hegira then followed in the wake of the mail truck. The idlers who had watched the train come in now moved on to the post office to wait for the mail to be put up, but, make no mistake, Newton always said, the depot was the hub of all this activity.

It ceased when they stopped the trains and took up the tracks. Things were just never the same again. Newton had loved that depot and used to mourn its closing. He told me there was never again a daily ritual in which all of Fayetteville participated; that the time was gone when you could see people from all over town, rich and poor, old and young, black and white, congregated at the same place and visiting with each other. He was right.

Huey Nipper eventually bought the depot. He had a grocery store in the waiting room on the lower level and a restaurant, three steps up, where the station master's office and the storage room had been. He served dinner six days a week. He put out a meat, three vegetables, bread, ice tea and dessert for a dollar and a quarter, all cooked fresh that day. Huey didn't believe in serving canned goods. He drew a big crowd and was a local institution, but Newton said it just wasn't the same feeling as when the train used to run.

I had been raised out in the county and lacked the emotional ties to the depot that my friend experienced. The depot at Woolsey, the closest town to my home, was seven miles down the track from Fayetteville and only about one-third as big a building. My friend Joe-Joe's daddy was the station master, and I can remember that the little depot sat high on underpinnings to be level with the tracks and that Mr. Tommy had a vegetable garden out back. Once they formed a Woman's Club in Woolsey and tried to have a little park in front of the depot with a bench and a path and some flowers. It never amounted to much and only the wisteria outlasted the short-lived organization. All the women went back to the Baptist Missionary Society and studied Paul and Lottie Moon.

You could sneak up on the platform at Woolsey and hear bumblebees humming under the overhang and the telegraph key jumping and chattering away while Mr. Tommy hoed in his garden, paying the telegraph no more mind than he did the bees. The closest personal association I ever had with the depot was certainly a vicarious one.

Joe-Joe's momma had a flower pit with a concrete bottom that would hold a little rain water for a week or so after a summer shower, and one June Joe-Joe and I found the bottom of that pit covered with toad frogs that had jumped in and couldn't jump out. We got sacks and collected them. There must have been more than two hundred frogs there. We rationed ourselves in collection of trophies; I carried twenty home with me and Joe-Joe gathered thirty, since it was his momma's flower pit.

This was about the time the Japanese were beginning to experiment with cultured pearls, and I had read a story about inserting a grain of sand in the oyster's shell and later garnering a gem. I had a mind with what I fancied was a scientific bent, audacity belying my appearance and visionary tendencies undreamt by my family and peers. I made a small incision in each frog's belly, inserted a grain of sand, closed the incision with sewing thread and dreamed of "Hoppy-toad Pearls from Woolsey, Georgia," such gorgeous pearls that New York socialites would be clamoring for them. I would be wealthy, famous, handsome and very generous; I dreamed of empire. Every one of my frogs died within two weeks.

Not so Joe-Joe's. He not only lacked any consuming desire for fame and fortune; he was also downright squeamish about messing around with hoppy-toads. He believed in warts. He asked what to do with his frogs. I knew that my aunt was going to Atlanta on the day following our unexpected harvest. She was not the most popular member of our family, nor did she enjoy universal affection in the community. She "put on airs," always an error in a village where everyone knows all your kin for at least two generations back. When Joe-Joe puzzled about what to do with his sack of thirty frogs, I suggested that if it was at all possible for him to remain undetected, he should snitch my aunt's suitcase in the waiting room the next morning when she arrived at the depot and distribute the lively frogs throughout its contents. By some delicious chain of happenstance, Joe-Joe was able to do exactly that.

My unsuspecting aunt opened her grip in the prestigious home of her hostess in Atlanta, and Joe-Joe's thirty warty frogs scrambled to freedom, hopping and peeing with excitement. Apparently my aunt and her hostess emulated the activity of the frogs. I learned of the success of the venture when my aunt returned a week later and came to our house for a private audience with my grandmother. Upon her departure, with no questions asked, no evidence presented, my grandmother carried me to the side yard, made me roll up my overalls and proceeded to stripe my legs stingingly with a peach-tree switch. No one ever suspected Joe-Joe.

Newton Gaddis had closer association and warmer personal memories of his depot in Fayetteville. The train blew for Harp's Crossing, but the next scheduled stop going south was the town of Inman, labeled Ackert in contradiction on the side of the railroad station. Newton liked to tell about the evening when he was on the loading platform as the train began chugging out for Inman after disgorging its passengers and mail in Fayetteville. As the last car went sliding slowly by, Newton was amazed to see Betsill Cox ensconced on the observation platform, tilted back in a chair with his brogans propped on the railing, sockless shanks gleaming like churn dashers.

Betsill was a fifty-year-old bachelor who made a little shine when he had to have groceries but lived reclusively in a one-room shack at the end of a winding trail somewhere in the woods between Inman and Woolsey. Although Newton had not been living in our county long enough to be sure who all was kin to whom, he had been there long enough to have learned to keep his mouth shut until he was sure. He was familiar with all the local characters and he cherished them. He knew that I was not related to either the Coxes or the Betsills, and therefore it was all right to talk to me. To Newton's knowledge, Betsill Cox had never even been to church or a funeral, and certainly had never set foot outside Fayette County before.

"Betsill, " he hailed, "where in the big, bright, ever-loving, blue-eyed world have you been, Son?"

"Been to Atlanta, Mr. Gaddis. Been to Atlanta all day long, by God."

Newton walked the platform apace with the moving train.

"What all did you do, Betsill, in Atlanta?" He had to trot a little to keep up as the Inman-bound chain of cars speeded up.

"Went through the five-and-dime, saw a moving picture show called *Birth of a Nation* that made me mad as hell, et at a fancy restaurant called S & W and spent the afternoon in a whorehouse on Whitehall Street."

By now, the train was leaving Newton Gaddis behind. He reached the end of the platform and hollered at the man disappearing down the track on the observation platform.

"How'd you manage all that in one day, Betsill?"

Betsill Cox arose from his chair and leaned over the railing. He cupped his hands around his mouth and responded.

"Kinfolks!" he yelled. "Kinfolks, by God!"

Perhaps Newton Gaddis was right. Perhaps depots were the social hubs of the rural America of his day. I sure understand why he loved them so.

JIM HARRISON

SAINT ROXIE

IF ANYONE who grew up on a farm before 1940 pauses long enough in the presence of a No. 3 galvanized tub, soon or late he will be inundated with memories of Monday. If Sunday was dedicated to godliness, Monday, in turn, was devoted to cleanliness. Usually, the washplace was on the lee-side of the smokehouse or tacked onto a shed. There was a crudely constructed platform of rough-sawn boards jutting out from the building at mid-thigh level to conserve the backs of women in their cadence of bend and stoop and lift. The side of the building had nails that held the tubs when they were not in use and also the scrub board. The batterstick, bleached out and puffy, was usually just propped up on the washbench; batter-sticks were easy to come by.

Exactly three steps from the washbench was the ember-strewn mound where the washpots rested, rolled on their sides and black as soot, crusty on the outside and glossy smooth on the inside. They had three stubby little sharp-pointed legs that balanced them on precisely placed bricks when they were in use. A washpot was of a roundness and fullness not duplicated today except by the bottoms and bellies of some ladies who stroll Six Flags unaware that they, with the aid of stretch knit, have managed to mimic the contour of the old-fashioned washpot.

The washpots were used for boiling clothes. They were of cast-iron to withstand the tremendous heat of lightwood knots and pine wood burning directly around and under them. They lasted forever. Washing was not their only function. They were used in the wintertime at hog killing to render lard. White slick cubes were cut from the blanket of fat insulating a well-fed, freshly slaughtered adult hog, piled into the washpot and boiled. A hissing, blubbering cauldron of liquid, as clear as any olive oil, sent its steam and fragrance into the winter air, the cubes themselves shrinking up into crisp and tiny morsels called cracklings, which gave promise of gourmet bread to be eaten with winter greens. The lard was ready as soon as the cracklings were done. They were dipped out with a strainer and the molten grease poured up into five-gallon cans, always new and clean. When chilled, it firmed up into the snow-white lard that was the basic ingredient of Southern cooking in the days before cholesterol and was lidded tightly for storage in the smokehouse.

Later in the week, when women had time to get around to it, the trash fat, trimmed from the hogs' chitterlings and other places, unsuitable for rendering into lard, was cooked in the same washpot, with wood ashes, for conversion into soap. Red Devil Lye was also used as a saponifying aid. The lye came in a small can with the crimson image of a horned devil leering on it, complete with pitchfork, barbed tail and leaping flames. The sparkling crystalline substance sizzled and smoked when added to water. No rural community was free of at least one horror story of a small child being burned with lye and permanently disfigured by scars or blindness. There has never been more graphic warning or truth in advertising than the label on that can, but some infants even drank the caustic chemical instead of just pulling it over on themselves.

The soap, when done, was a bland, bleached-out tan color and was stored in any old container with much less care than the lard. This soap was not used for bathing but was cut into semi-rigid cakes and used for scouring floors and washing dirty clothes. No perfume was added, but lye soap emitted its own distinctive fragrance. The smell of no other soap in all the world has ever evoked the image of "clean" so vividly as boiled-in-the-washpot, almost-soft lye soap.

Every Monday in the washplaces of the South, the pots were filled with water drawn by hand from the well. A truly well-built fire had the water singing and rolling in short order, and the dirty clothes were dumped in. Chunks and shavings of lye soap were added, and the clothes were boiled and boiled and boiled. The washerwoman pushed them down into the pot over and over with an old well-rounded stick as trapped bubbles of air raised them from the cleansing froth.

The steaming, sodden clothes were lifted on the end of a stick and transported to an upended, hardwood stump placed by the washbench. Here, they were flailed and turned and flailed again with the batterstick, then tossed into the first tub. This one contained the scrub board, a corrugated rectangle of galvanized metal supported by a wooden frame. The clothes, after being beaten, were rubbed vigorously and bumpily up and down the scrub board and then transported through the next two tubs in sequence of rinsing. Finally they were squeezed and twisted to wring them free of excess water. Carried to the clothesline, shaken out and fastened with wood clothespins onto smoothly stretched wire, they sunned and flapped to fragrant dryness. They smelled of wind and sun as well as lye soap. Clothes may not have lasted long in the South, but by every Monday afternoon they were the cleanest in all the world.

All of this frenzied activity had to be finished in time for the women to have dinner on the table when the men came in from the fields. If the rural South had not been overwhelmingly

Protestant, some determined, bent-backed, rapidly moving, indestructible washerwoman would have been beatified early on so that farmers' wives would have had their own saint on wash day. Somehow, it never seemed to me that Jesus was quite adequate on Monday mornings. Mary got the blessing, but chances are it was Martha who washed the clothes.

All farm families have their memories of the washplace, of Monday morning, but I think my wife's grandmother was the most likely candidate for sainthood in that department. It may take another hundred years or so for the remembrances of her to be smoothed and softened enough, but she deserves it; she could quite capably fill the role.

I never saw her. She lived and died three hundred miles and ten years from my awareness, but I know her. So vivid is her memory among her descendents, so real her legend in her native community, that I have the same reverence, respect, affection and fear that she engendered in all of them. Her genes swim in my wife and my children and are awesome when they surface. It will wear a man out just to behold them.

Her name was Roxie. She was born into the farming culture of northwest Florida after The War, but wasted little time either pondering the privilege of gentle birth or bemoaning the loss of previous opulence. Roxie was a pioneer woman but did not have to leave home to be one. She would have been a pioneer no matter where she was. She took fate by the scruff of the neck, shook it into a shape that suited her, and went vigorously about her business, her family in her train. Reconstruction may have been overwhelming the South, but it was of peripheral concern to her. Reconstruction to Roxie was an active pursuit of her own, an opportunity to change people and events that fell short of her expectations.

She snatched up the threads of southern sun, long-leaf pines, sandy fields, cypress-stained creeks, Federal oppression, Baptist morality, hard labor; laid them all into the loom of family pride with inflexible opinion; and wove a tapestry that will endure for ages. She asked no mercy; she made her way.

Roxie married a man as well connected as she. He was named Badger, a pleasant man, friendly, tolerant and easygoing. They sent all their sons to college and graduate school from a farm in Gadsden County, Florida, before shade tobacco made the area prosperous. If they felt this a boastful accomplishment, they never let on; they just kept working and going to church. Roxie's supervising eye never flickered.

One Monday in her youth, she was at the washplace. The recurring trips to the washpot, the pounding block, the scrub board and the rinsing tub were rhythmically under way. She had broken a sweat and was competently disposing of Monday. Over the fence in the adjacent sandy field, Badger was steadily plowing corn. The lark was on the wing, and all was right with Roxie's world. In unexpected reversal, the snail became impaled on the thorn.

Badger had a visitor. A neighbor from a distant farm came by in his wagon and hailed him. While Roxie worked, Badger whoa-ed his mule and propped on the handle of his plowstock, feet crossed in a fresh-turned furrow as he ignored the unplowed corn and visited with his friend. Courtesy was a cardinal virtue to Badger.

Roxie's step became faster; she beat the work pants more vigorously; she scrubbed in a frenzy with elbows high. The visit continued. Roxie poked her boiling clothes so hard that water spilled over and hissed in the hot ashes. Still Badger played the role of the gracious host in the cornfield, neighborly and cordial.

Roxie endured it as long as she could. She flung a stickload of clothes from the pot into the scrubbing tub and stepped with purpose to the fence. She cupped her hands around her mouth, never acknowledging the neighbor's presence.

"Badger!" she bellowed. "You, Badger! You keep that mule a-turning!"

St. Roxie! I love the sound of it. Realistic, reconstructing Roxie! Symbolic as the Phoenix. Manipulating matriarch! Directive doyenne! St. Roxie of the Washplace! Sainthood has been conferred on less deserving figures.

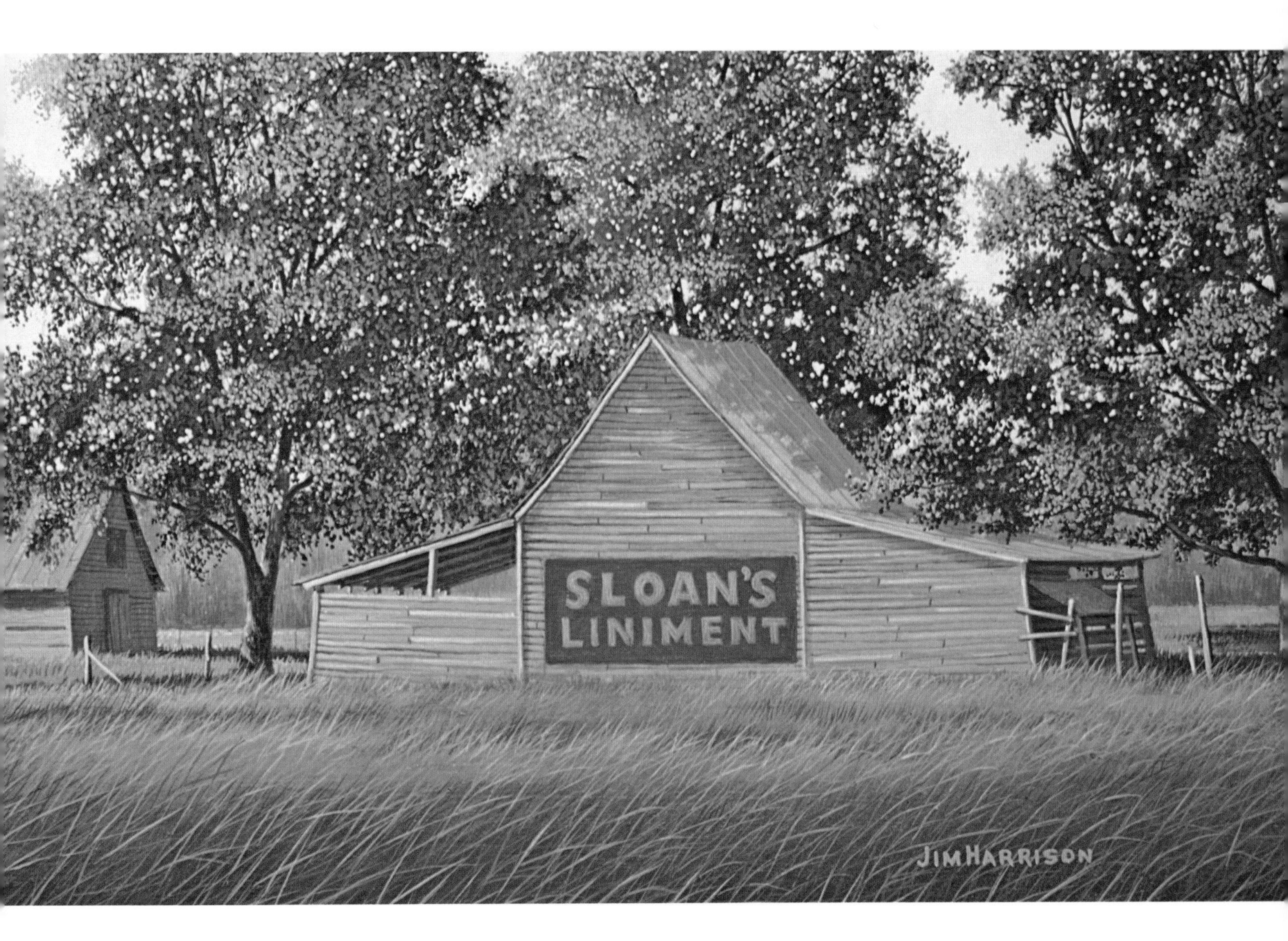
SLOAN'S
LINIMENT
JIMHARRISON

JIM HARRISON

THE BIG ROAD

ROADS are a wonder now. The downtown connector in Atlanta is like a carefully crafted necklace snuggling the neck of a lovely woman; it accents the beauty of the buildings it encircles. Where else can one behold a marble cube floating back-lit in the evening sky? A Capitol dome glistening gold? A pink granite garden of Babylon towering in stair-step silhouette? A cylinder of shining mirrors shafting higher than them all, to its right a blue toadstool with a revolving restaurant in the top? Nestling incongruously in the heart of them all, at the foot of the skyscrapers, a Negro church maintains its sturdy steeple, adorned with a neon cross and the bright blue message that "JESUS SAVES." It is almost a cautioning wail. He who has ears to hear, let him hear; eyes to see, let him see.

Fast following through the brain, however, comes rolling the age old question, "What is man that thou art mindful of him?" One looks at Grady Hospital, the Peachtree Plaza hotel, the Georgia Pacific Building, considers the Tom Moreland Interchange to the north on I-85 and exults, "For thou has made him only a little lower than the angels." Jesus Saves, indeed, but from within a challenging conglomerate of heritage and accomplishment.

Roads are no accident. When I was little, I puzzled over the terminology of my grandfather. He referred to "the road," "the big road," "the public road," "back roads," and, rarely, "the hard road." Early in the settlement of our county, a man himself had to keep up the road by his own house and farm. In addition, he had to donate so many hours of labor or else pay a road tax in order to maintain the public roads and the big road. Later, when progress had produced enough criminals to justify the expense of chain gangs, the roads were worked, ditches cleaned and bridges built by prisoners at county expense. The back roads were neglected. They were scraped maybe once a year, maybe not. Trees leaned over them, their branches touching in mingled green arch, or else sunlight on the open stretches ripened bountiful crops of berries and plums.

The feel of a country road beneath bare feet made an Antaeus of each of us. Instant awareness of place and time came through that contact. One knew the time of day by the touch of the road coming up through padding feet. Cool and moist in early morning, scorching sand or baking clay at noon, warm and comforting as the shadows lengthened into late afternoon, the country road contributed to our being part of our universe and to our being in control of it; we could conquer kingdoms while walking on a country road.

Passage on the road in those days was a simple matter of people occasionally going from one place to another. It was so infrequent and sporadic that a black runner might sun himself an hour or a bobwhite kick in wallowing ectasy as he fluffed and dusted his feathers or a box terrapin have time to dig a nest and deposit her eggs in an unpacked stretch on the shoulder. Not a road in the county was paved, and travel was a leisurely process.

Eventually the road connecting Harp's Crossing and Inman and Woolsey to Fayetteville on one end and Griffin on the other became the big road. It was widened and graded and, some time in the dim future, it might even be paved. People did not worry about that; they were too happy to get what improvements they could. Farmers gave the necessary amount of land for the road willingly, with the exception of one, who demanded recompense and went to court with condemnation proceedings. The jury awarded him one dollar, and the stain of greed was ever thereafter on his escutcheon.

Not so Mr. John Burch. He owned the biggest farm on the road and lived in the biggest house. He was the first to sign over a right-of-way, becoming a symbol of community support for all others to emulate. Many years later when automobiles had multipled like cockroaches and drivers took to giving hand signals on turning, for reasons of safety rather than just neighborly information, the Georgia State Patrol was founded. About twice a month one of its officers would even go by the Burch homestead, traversing the dusty thoroughfare that was now known as State Highway 92 rather than the Woolsey-Inman Road.

Mr. Burch and his wife were long dead. His middle daughter, Miss Sadie, lived there and looked after her younger sister, Miss Fannie Mae. Miss Sadie had never married, not from lack of choice but because of dedication to more self-effacing demands. She cared for both her aging parents until their departures from this world. The sons of Brother Walter, who had built across the road, performed tasks for her that exceeded the capacity of a lady. The chief commitment in her life, however, was to Miss Fannie Mae.

The younger sister had asthma and had been dying since the day she was born. At age fifty, she looked eighty, weighed all of seventy-five pounds, and had sucked so hard for every breath that her collar bones rose up almost to her chin. One upper eyelid drooped perpetually at half-mast, and she constantly clutched a handkerchief in her little bird claw of a hand. She was purple. When she was sixty, she told Miss Sadie in the springtime that it was worth staying alive just to smell the lilacs, but it took her five minutes to get the words out. Miss Sadie did not cry; she wondered aloud to a neighbor in slow, inflectionless speech if paving the road some day and getting rid of the dust might not help Fannie Mae's asthma.

I never saw Miss Sadie weep. She was the calmest, most self-possessed person I remember from my childhood. She was also one of the most universally respected. She played piano for the Methodist Church at Inman, Mr. John Burch having been able to provide considerable cultural advantages for his daughters in their youth. Her voice was dry; it always sounded a little cracked. She spoke slowly and then only after deliberate consideration. To my Woolsey-Baptist perception, she was a Methodist saint, a John Wesley nun, a Southern lady, approachable but untouchable.

One morning she left her sister in the back sitting room, ensconced in a wing chair, pulling the edges of her handkerchief repetitively between her fingers. Miss Fannie Mae liked to stay busy, and that was about the only activity left that she could muster the energy to perform. It was not a fruitful, but a comforting, endeavor. Miss Sadie had to run out to Miss Nannie's store to get a few things.

As she backed into Highway 92 and headed her A-Model Ford toward Inman, a state patrolman happened by and stopped his patrol car in her path.

"Lady!" he admonished. "You can't do that!"

Miss Sadie enjoyed the security not only of being a maiden daughter in the Burch family but also of decades of perpetually correct behavior. She looked at the officer with calm politeness.

"I can't do what, young man?"

"You can't just back out into the middle of a state highway, plumb across to the other side of the big road like that!"

Miss Sadie gave his statement brief consideration, sniffed once editorially and replied in dry, even tones, without passion but with considerable conviction.

"I don't for the life of me see why not, young man. Papa gave the road."

The road is paved now. The oak grove around the Burch place has been cut down, the wraparound porches removed; automobiles speed by at fantastic speeds and in prodigious numbers. I wonder, could Papa see it now, if he would still give the land.

When I ride the Atlanta connector with cars traveling six abreast in both directions, I marvel at how far we have come from the dirt roads of our past. I consider the legal tangles and time involved in right-of-way acquisition, and I wonder whose Papa gave this land.

I recall the dirt roads as I regard the concrete caverns and the temples of prosperity. What indeed is man? Is this work of the hands of man, that we designate our capital city, to be equated with progress? Is He who made us only a little lower than the angels mindful also of Atlanta?

The calm statement glows in blue neon.

"JESUS SAVES."

I hope it is true.

JIM HARRISON

AR GRIND
MAXWE
HOUS
Good to the
NET WT
JIM HARRISON

THE MANSION

LIGHTNING lived in an unpainted house that had three rooms. There was a bedroom for him and his wife and daughter, a lean-to for his sons, and the stove room where they cooked and ate and entertained whatever visitors who came around. It may have been a cabin, but it was not a shack. They covered the inside walls with cardboard to insulate against winter winds. Lightning's wife, in addition, plastered the stove room with layers of colored comic pages garnered from years of cleaning up and toting off at the Big House.

Lightning did not tolerate anyone's tearing loose boards off his house to start a fire, and his wife did not allow anyone to track mud across her floors. The house did not belong to them, but they lived in it for thirty years and thought it did. When something wore out, Lightning patched it. His wife was fond of saying, "Be neat. Be clean. And have a little talk with Jesus every day." She would scold a little and laugh a lot. The house responded.

It stood alone on the crest of the field. It was so near the Big House that Lightning kept his mule in the Bossman's barn; his wife's milk cow was likewise allowed to shelter there. The only outbuildings around Lightning's house were the well with its time-slicked log for windlass and the privy, which crouched well below the crest of the field on the edge of the sweetgum thicket and had a croker sack for a door.

Years of rain pouring off the tin roof of the house packed the red clay yard, and over time the drip line settled down and away from the foundation stones. The sills, in turn, canted toward the center, giving the impression that the house grew there, that it was rooted.

Lightning's folks all laughed more than they grumbled. There were plenty of things about which to do either, and they chose the high road. Instead of grumbling that there were no screens at the windows, they laughed about the old hen that flew in and laid an egg slap in the middle of Maw's bed. The entire family addressed the business of living; they worked hard enough never to fear hunger. Then they worked even harder hoping to get a little ahead, which was another matter altogether.

Every first Sunday they went to church. Lightning never owned a car, and they walked two miles through the woods. They left at ten and stayed all day. The children went to school from November through March and an additional month in August when the cotton was laid by but had not yet opened. The school went only through the seventh grade, and most children dropped out before then, either yielding to the pressures of puberty or fleeing the academic tyranny of Miss Willie, who was a stern disciplinarian and wore flowing scarves to hide the white spots on her neck. Lightning's children all finished the local pyramid of learning.

They grew up, married, farmed, visited their parents on Sundays, went to war. Lightning grew old and was able to plow only half a day and knock about a little. The Bossman helped establish his age and gave him a pension. Lightning died first and later his wife. One of their grandsons went to the University on a football scholarship and studied law. A great-granddaughter works in the bank. Lightning did not live to see either.

The house stood empty for years because the Bossman could not stand to see anyone else live in it. Even when the chinaberry trees grew up all around it, you could still tell that Lightning had lived there. Paint, when all is said and all is done, may be nothing more than a badge of privilege.

JIM HARRISON

CHEW
MAIL POUCH
TOBACCO
TREAT YOURSELF TO THE BEST
JIM HARRISON

BE STILL AND KNOW

WHEN A church appears in a painting, it comprises a focus, an accent, the appeal of which is universal. Monet portrayed the Cathedral at Rouen unforgettably. Rockefeller gave us the restored Rose Window at Rheims. Notre Dame rules the Isle de la Cité in Paris. It is breath catching to behold across the plains surrounding Chartres the cathedral spires that rise up and point toward God. St. Paul's is the very heart of London. The unfinished National Cathedral in Washington is the pride of the capital. All of these magnificent landmarks of worship have appeared in numerous paintings and are widely familiar.

Granting them their grandeur and majesty, confessing the awe they inspire, none of these world-famous churches, however, quite warms the human spirit and strikes the chord of memory like the sight of a small church in an American landscape. Nearly every person of my generation has a feeling of security, of serenity, engendered by the spire of a church against the skyline of a village. Second only to praise of the autumn leaves are the comments I hear about the churches in New England.

Our churches in the South are just as important to us; more often than not, they are the center of communal life for their members. Not all the memories they evoke, however, are reverential. Comedy frequently attends tragedy, and there is a resistant streak not far below the surface in some humans that makes them rebel against total immersion in the sacred. Memories of church attendance are therefore not uniformly tranquil and benevolent. Something can always happen that triggers our ebullient sense of the ridiculous and forces us to laugh in the presence of piety. These events also contribute to the richness of our recall when we see a painting of a church.

I was reared in an era when children should be seen and not heard. Nowhere was this more evident than on Sunday morning in church. It has been a trifle difficult, therefore, for me to adjust to the interruptions of ritual throughout our land called Children's Worship. It has been almost universally adopted over the last decade, even in churches with thick carpet on the floor, gleaming accouterments on the Communion table, highly polished altar rails complete with velvet cushions and formal order of worship imprinted on bulletins handed out by ushers as overly hospitable as attendants at a mortuary. The appellation is incorrect. The event may be worship of the children by preening parents and doting grandparents, but it is most certainly not children's worship. They are not worshiping.

Neither is anyone else for that five minutes. To have a preacher try to reduce the gospel to the level of a three- or four-year-old, and usually in a patronizing tone from a posture calculatedly reminiscent of the Master when He beckoned the children to come unto Him, fills me with foreboding. I cannot help wondering if the minister may not be preparing to spoon-feed me also some simplistic, overly reduced approach to religion when my turn comes. I squirm until Children's Worship is done, and I ponder new connotations for Christ's use of the word *suffer*. Christianity is so full of it.

There is one Children's Worship I am sorry I missed, however. It occurred in a metropolitan church of some opulence, and of even more sophistication. There was a great bevy of small children clustered around the minister, who was sitting on the cushion of the altar rail. The little girls were smoothing their skirts, adjusting their hair, stealing covert glances at the dresses of the other little girls. The little boys were squirming self-consciously, their angelic demeanor a result of their aware-

JIM HARRISON

ness of what their mothers had threatened to do to them if they picked their noses.

With arms outstretched and encircling several of the small worshipers, the minister asked in a folksy tone designed to encourage participation, "Which one of you children can tell me this morning what has sharp little teeth, soft gray fur and runs up and down tree trunks in the woods?"

He was met with silence, most of the children searching for the cautionary eyes of their parents, oblivious to the expectant hush of their audience.

The minister persisted. "I'll give you another clue. It has a long bushy tail and likes to eat nuts for breakfast. Who wants to tell me what I'm talking about?"

Still there was attention but no responses. He enticed, he wheedled. "Oh, come on now. Surely at least one of you can tell me what that is."

On the periphery of the group, a four-year-old boy, his tolerance for Children's Worship probably already limited to less than one more year, took a long, shuddering breath and spoke loudly and intrepidly.

"I know we're supposed to say 'Jesus,' but it sure sounds like a squirrel to me."

I have encountered no other raison d'être so cogent, and, ever since, I suffer Children's Worship without irritation.

Even funerals can produce mirth. I was not present, but there was a funeral that has been legend in our community, and I have heard of it from several participants. The account is so standard that I believe it to be true. It occurred in the local A.M.E. Church on the edge of town.

Gil Cooper was a member of one of the oldest families in our county, one with multiple members and with solid respectability. Gil was a bit of a maverick in the family but was accepted with tolerance and love. He never married, his love of alcohol and social excesses interfered with steady employment, and he died at a relatively early age. Chronologically.

The community turned out for the funeral, in support of the family as well as in manifestation of Christian communion in the presence of death. On the very front row sat Gil's maiden sister, Birdie Belle. She was older than he, had never drawn other than a sober breath, but was also a bit of an eccentric in her own right. She, too, had never married. She was a tiny little woman of birdlike thinness, her aging skin as free of blemishes and wrinkles as that of a baby. She was known across the county as a person of unshakable affability, her greetings to everyone as cordial and spontaneous as those of an enthusiastic and friendly child. She gave little of her attention to politics, civil rights, the rapidly improving lot of the Negro in our society. She was what she was. Everywhere. With everybody. People said it was hard to make her mad.

The day they buried Gil was an exception; she got mad. She got mad at the preacher, and she let him know about it, when it happened and where it happened. The A.M.E. Reverend took advantage of the large attendance at the funeral for more than a little exhortation. In fact, he preached a complete sermon and had worked himself into a sweat and his congregation into participatory responses of "Yes, Lord" and "Amen" whenever he paused for rhythmic breaths.

After reaching the climax of what he regarded as one of his more successful homiletic endeavors in our town, he finally came to the eulogy. He looked down at the open casket.

"Dearly beloved, we come to bury this brother in Christ!"

"Yes, Lord."

"As our Master said when He walked this earth, we come to bury brother Gil, not to praise him!"

"Amen."

"We speak in the house of the Lord, and we speak with the tongue of angels and truth and not with the lying forked tongue of the devil!"

"Yes, Lord."

"Now, we all of us assembled here today know that brother Gil was not all that he could have been or should have been."

The amens fell off a little.

"We recognize the fact, dearly beloved, that brother Gil wouldn't hold a job or come to church."

The audience response, in the face of editorial comment on truth this current, was definitely dwindling. There were only scattered murmurs of "Yes, Lord."

The reverend stormed into crescendo to regain the group rapport. He stomped a foot in the pulpit, crashed a meaty hand, palm down, on the lectern and roared.

"We all know, children of the living God, that brother Gil was bad to lay out, and skin, and drink liquor, and run after fallen women!"

From her seat on the front row, directly in front of the casket, Birdie Belle rose to her tiny height, black straw hat riding precariously atop her fluffed-out, unbraided hair, dressed with great care in unaccustomed fashion for the special event of a family funeral. With consuming indignation, she manifested pride of clan and the loyalty of a faithful sister.

"That's a damn lie!" she shrieked. The church stilled. Totally. Birdie Belle doubled up her tiny little fist, stepped forward and shook it upward at the preacher. Into her background she reached for the most effective threat she could recall.

"If you don't hush your mouth this minute, I'm going to put the white folks on you! You infernal black leg of Satan, you!"

She whirled and marched with long strides up the aisle, swinging her pocketbook by the handle, lips poked out, looking to neither side, unaware that her hat had skewed rakishly over one ear. Birdie Belle later told my older sister, "White woman, way I look at it, a sinner got just as much right in Heaven as anybody else."

There was a considerable exodus in her wake. The members of the A.M.E. Church could not break tradition enough to laugh at a funeral in the church house, with the coffin open. They needed air.

Across town, the minister of the Methodist Episcopal Church

South also had problems with a funeral. He had been in our community for only two weeks and, indeed, was so new-come to the ministry itself that he had not yet recognized that people in small towns condone little but forgive much, even in their preachers. He was precipitated into an identity crisis that revolved around church policy, Christian doctrine and the even more threatening question of personal ministerial dignity. The county's only Republican died, and the new preacher was called on to bury him.

The deceased did not like anybody in town very much, a fact that may have been cause as well as result of his political condition. He did, however, adore his fox terrier and carried him with him wherever he went. Several years before, the little dog had died and the grieving master had embalmed and interred him in one corner of the chicken house, awaiting his own death, at which time he proclaimed that the beloved animal was to be buried at his grieving master's feet. Intimately. Within the coffin itself. The town knew of this eccentricity but paid little attention to it. After all, the man was a Republican.

It was said the widow chose the Methodist church for the funeral not because either she or her husband had ever attended it but because it was recently air-conditioned. The new preacher properly, if a little awkwardly, did his best at consoling the newly bereaved wife, who was also such a new acquaintance for him. He assured her that he would tailor the service to her desires, including selection of scripture and hymns. She was dully appreciative but left those matters to the preacher. Her interest lay elsewhere.

"Preacher, what did you say your name was? Well, Preacher, Jack is embalmed and buried in the chicken house where it couldn't rain on him, waiting for this day and his final resting place. I promised my husband we'd dig him up and bury him in the coffin with him. You don't mind that, do you?"

The new preacher murmured that if any problem was posed by this request, the undertaker could solve it handily. A few minutes later, he consulted a member of his Board of Stewards.

"I didn't know that couple had a child. How old was little Jack when he died?"

The steward set the minister straight. The minister was aghast.

"A dog? A dog? Man, I can't preach a funeral, let alone my very first one in town, with a dog in the casket! I'm a Methodist minister, a Christian minister, and, besides, what would the DS and the Bishop say if they ever heard about it? Man, I'm not about to make myself a laughing stock! I'm not going to have a funeral service over a dog!"

The steward was a bit of a wag and had seen preachers come and seen preachers go. He soberly assured this one that they were not confronting a matter of life and death, so to speak.

"Don't be so stubborn, preacher. Relax. Look at what a great opportunity this is. You have it within your grasp to make ecclesiastical history. Don't pass it by."

"What do you mean?"

"For the first time in the history of the Methodist Church, or any other church, I strongly suspect, you can stand up in that pulpit and in perfectly correct English, without being accused of cussing, you can say to the congregation, 'Beloved in Christ, I want to talk to you today about the son of a bitch in this coffin.'"

The steward was not only a wag but an ardent Democrat. The preacher relaxed into weak but dismissing laughter.

Jack was neither eulogized nor mentioned at the funeral. The only person who ever knew for sure whether or not he was in the casket was Harry Redwine, the undertaker. The minister left town after his tour of duty and always stoutly maintained that Jack was not in there.

The town was skeptical. What did preachers know? Besides, Harry was the one who had final access and also the one who looked to the widow for payment of his bill.

Harry recognized valuable attention when it was bestowed upon him, and he never told. Not even when Neal Dettmering or Kate Greer in later years would buy him a drink at the Elk's Club and try to pry it out of him. Harry went to his own grave twenty-five years later with the secret intact. Nobody knows for sure.

So. Although everyone can look at a church and recollect instances of hilarity, that is not the main memory the sight of one triggers. We have all grown up with the Burning Bush, with certain catch phrases, and we cannot rid ourselves of the heritage.

We look at a painting of a white church against a background of human endeavor or natural bounty, and we revert, even if only for a little while, to reverence.

Be still.

Be still and know.

Be still and know that I AM.

But you have to be very still.

Moses was.

JIM HARRISON

Gillette Safety Razor
NO STROPPING, NO HONING
SLOAN'S
LINAMENT
666 COLD TABLETS
10 2
Dr Pepper
4
JIM HARRISON

JIM HARRISON

THE WAGON

I CAME along well after the automobile began shrinking American distances, but the wagon was still universal. Not every family owned a car, but it was essential that every farm have a wagon. The wagon was used to haul guano to fresh furrows in April, cotton to the gin in October, corn to the crib in November, fodder from the fields in July, newly cut saplings to the wood lot in December.

Sometime in June, when the days had grown long and were singing with sun and Mr. Louis Kerlin could work a neighbor in, he would bring his binding machine to cut our ripened grain. It was drawn by mammoth horses instead of mules, their massive, rounded hooves festooned with bangs of curly hair. As soon as the dew dried off enough, that marvelous machine would flail and chatter inexorably through a field of oats or wheat, scattering mice, fee larks and coach whips in a panic, leaving stubble as uniform and stiff as the head of a boy in a barbershop.

A wagon followed the binder to carry the bound bundles of wheat to be shocked near the barn until the thresher could come. The bundles were always stacked on the wagon with the heavy heads of grain pointing in, so high and tight that the entire load swayed as a unit if the wagon ran over a pebble or turned a corner. No farmer could do without a wagon.

Some farmers laid boards across the sides or even put chairs in the wagon bodies to carry the family to town on Saturday or to church on Sunday, but that was a rough ride. Most people who could not afford an automobile still kept a buggy for travel, a more comfortable vehicle with a seat balanced on springs that afforded bounce instead of jolt. Buggies were frail and light, as tautly balanced as a buzzard's outstretched wing and every bit as black.

Mr. Ira White had the last buggy in Fayette County. Until the day he died, he drove it to town every Saturday and tied his horse at the courthouse square. He had droves of grandchildren who would have brought his groceries to him, but what was a self-respecting farmer to do with a Saturday if he did not spend it in town? Until well into the sixties he was generous about giving small children a ride, his silver hair gleaming in the dark interior of the buggy, perfect counterpoint to the white horse dressed out in black blinders and harnessed between the buggy shafts.

Mr. Quaker Davis said a good buggy was so tightly decked out that a fly could neither set down on it or leave without the driver knowing it. Mr. Quaker was the only man I ever met who had known my grandfather when he was growing up. He always told me the same story when we visited, his eyes twinkling and his words tumbling out in such fast staccato that they fluttered his mustaches. Mr. Quaker was reputed to disdain dentists and to pull his own teeth with pliers when they troubled him. I believed the legend. He had left a few; they contributed to the individuality of his speech.

"Law, boy, your grandpa was a mess; in fact, he was a plumb sight. Let me tell you what kind of a fella he was. If you was setting on your front porch and he had a quarrel with you, he wouldn't ask you to step out in the road to settle nothing. He'd git off his horse, climb over the fence, snatch you off your own front porch and thrash you good. Then he'd shake hands with you and laugh, and that would be the end of it. That's the kind of man Jim Sams was.

"I recollect one time before any of us had gotten married there was a bunch of us laying out and frolicking around in the woods one day. It was on top of the hill, the other side of Bennett's Mill where the road run flat for a pretty good piece. We had all had a dram or two and the whole world was funny, but I don't guess you know about that.

"Here come Mr. Bobby Lee Cleveland, dressed up spic and span, taking his wife to see her Pa. He had married one of old man Grinning John Adams's gals. This county was covered up with John Adamses. There was Big John, Little John, Grinning John and Smiling John that I knowed of, and there may have been others. Grinning John loved watermelons. They was taking him one that Mr. Bobby Lee had grown, and it was so big it might nigh filled the trap on the back of the buggy. Must have weighed close on to fifty pound.

"We watched them pass, and Jim Sams bet us all a drink that he could steal that watermelon without Mr. Bobby Lee knowing it. He took off his shoes and rolled his britches legs up and went prancing and tipping behind that buggy with his shoulders all drawed up, and terectly here he come back with the melon. We all laid real quiet till we heard the buggy cross the bridge at the foot of the hill.

"Then we laughed till we rolled on the ground. Everbody said your grandpa was a sight. They said Jim Sams was so slick he could steal the shortening out of a cake and never break the crust."

The wagons are gone. So are the buggies. Ira White and Quaker Davis and Bobby Lee Cleveland and Grinning John Adams are gone. So is my grandfather.

In the bustling prosperity of Fayette County today, it is hard to catch their voices or raise their images. If you slow up enough around the courthouse square or on one of the few remaining dirt roads in the county, however, it can still be done.

If you slow up enough.

GROVES
CHILL
TONIC
JIM HARRISON

SHRINE
CIRCUS
SEPT
4-5-6
JIMHARRISON

HOLLOW-TAIL

A LONG time ago, it was not uncommon to ride along a narrow dirt road and come upon a home place where the barn was on one side and the dwelling house on the other. Usually, this was a one- or a two-horse farm, and the barn was a fairly intimate structure. A man added onto his barn with sheds when he prospered and his head of stock increased to where he needed to sprawl out and have more room. He added onto the house the same way when the babies kept coming along. Sheds on a barn gave a place a settled look.

The folks who lived in those houses weren't mindful much of views and panoramas. They didn't fret about what they could see out their front door; it looked pretty near the same all around. Everybody in the country didn't own an automobile in those days, and those who did had the grace to slow down in front of a man's house. They slowed enough not to raise a dust or run over the chickens or guineas that seemed to be forever in the middle of the big road if a car happened along. Or yet, an old dog would be lying there so mindful that this was his place and so sure of himself that he moved slow as cream rising to give a car passage between the ditches. You didn't see dead possums every mile or so in those days, squashed flat with crows pecking at their eyeballs and other goodies. It was generally a slower time. Nobody has time to slow down nowadays for an old possum to waddle out of the way, and it has been a long time since I have seen a flock of guineas. Macadam and the V-8 engine sure gave a zip to rural America.

Maude was raised across the road from her daddy's barn. Both structures were jam-up close to the road. She says you could smell the cow lot and the hog pen from the front porch and the outhouse from the back porch. You could also smell the honeysuckle and sweet shrub, the crabapple, the chinaberry where the chickens roosted and the mimosa, all of them as they came along in their season. It wasn't all bad, Maude said.

She was one of nine sisters; her folks didn't have any boys. Her daddy was old man Zedekiah Askew, and his daughters were raised in one bedroom. They stayed close all their lives. All of them married, every one of them just as soon as she could, and most of them lived to be eighty. They were always referred to in the county, no matter who they married or how old they got to be, as the Askew girls. They were a one generation monument to old man Zedekiah.

Of them all, Maude was the most practical. She could talk as flighty as any of them when it suited her, but all her sisters said that she really had a head on her shoulders. She married when she was seventeen and lived with the man three days, not long enough to set up housekeeping but plenty long enough to find out that "wedded bliss" was a misnomer insofar as she was concerned. The couple separated but did not divorce. They didn't need to; they both had a bellyful of wedlock.

Maude got herself a job in Atlanta. She worked at the ribbon counter in Woolworth's 5-&-10. She stayed in a rooming house on Pryor Street and came home on the train weekends when the weather wasn't too bad for somebody to meet her at the depot.

Her husband worked as a motorman on the streetcar in Atlanta. Every now and then Maude would have to ride on his car, but when she did, she never spoke. Neither did he. When she was twenty, a friend came by the five-and-dime and told Maude that her husband had been run over and killed by another streetcar when he was crossing the tracks at the car barn on his way to work.

Maude stopped long enough to buy herself a black hat with a

veil and went straight to the Georgia Power Company, where she created considerable disturbance in the business office. After that, she went to the funeral home and did as much grieving with her husband's mother as the old lady would let her do. They hadn't ever been what you could call close, Maude said. By the time the funeral was over and the mother got around to going to Georgia Power Company, Maude had the cash settlement and the pension and was set up for life. She never hit another lick at public work the longest day she lived. She framed her wedding certificate and hung it over her bed.

One time Maude contracted to buy a milk cow from the Watkins salesman who lived over the river. In later years, she'd tell the story to almost anybody who'd take the time to listen. Not a great many people heard it.

"That man represented that cow wrong to me in the first place. He said she give three gallon of milk a day and hadn't long been freshened. Well, sir, when he brought her to my place, she was in season already. I had to tie her in the stable and she bellowed all night long. On top of that, she had woofs in her back and was as gant and pore as an old suck-egg dog. I couldn't get but two and a half quarts from her, and I stripped her till we was both sore.

"Well, sir, I was not born yesterday, and when that old cow run off, I sent word to the Watkins man to come and get her, that I wasn't going to pay him for her. I couldn't throw twenty-five dollars away on a sorry critter what run off fore I'd had her twenty-four hours. I sent word at the same time for him to bring me a can of black pepper and a bottle of vanilla extract long as he was coming to my house anyway.

"I had the cash money ready for the pepper and the vanilla and thought maybe that would mollify him, but he was so tore up when he found the rope broke and the cow gone that there wasn't no reasoning with him. He hunted that cow a day and a half and never did find her, and, still and yet, he wanted me to pay for her.

"Well, sir, I wasn't about to do no such a fool thing as that, and you know what that Watkins man done? He sued me for that cow money, yes he did! When it was all over, I was so put out with him that I talked all the other ladies in the Corinth Baptist Church into boycotting Watkins products, and he spent I don't know how much on unnecessary gasoline before it come over him what we had done to him in our neck of the woods. You can't take advantage of a widow woman in our settlement and get away with it, I don't care who you are.

"But now I tell you one thing, sir, that's the first and only time I have ever been in a courtroom, and I don't aim never to get in another one if I live to be a hundred. I didn't have no lawyer, and I wasn't about to spend the money on one, and before it was over I got in a plumb sweat. It that judge hadn't of had a sense of humor on top of being a fine Christian gentleman, I ain't sure yet that I would have come clear.

"You know they make you swear on a Bible to tell the truth, the whole truth and nothing but the truth so help me God. Well, sir, that covers a heap of territory when you get to thinking about it, and the judge kept butting in and telling me to stick to the point. I told about the woofs in the back, and I even managed to tell about the cow being in season and the scant milk flow and all, and the judge just kept on boring in. He said, 'Miz Simpson, is that why the cow run away?'

"And I was mindful of the Bible and the swearing and all and I said, 'Judge, your honor, that old cow ain't worth telling a lie for. To tell the plumb stomp-down truth, she run away because she had the hollow-tail.'

"And the judge leaned over and he said to me, 'Did you say the hollow-tail?'

"You know that man, with college and law school and I don't know what all else behind him, hadn't never heard of the hollow-tail? He ast me what it was and I set in to tell him. 'Well Judge, your honor, sir,' I said, 'everybody raised on a farm around stock knows what hollow-tail is. When a cow gets it, her milk dries up and her bones stick out, and she won't eat and she keeps falling off 'til she gets down, and when a cow gets down, she dies. And the way you find the hollow-tail is to follow along the cow's tail from the top to the bottom 'til you come to a mushy place in it. It'll be two, three inches long, just as soft as can be, and that's where the hollow spot is and that's the hollow-tail.'

"He was still real interested and he said, 'Is this a fatal disease to the animal or is there a cure for it?'

"And I told him, sure, there's a cure if you got sense enough to think about the hollow-tail in the first place and look for it and find it, and that after I had squeezed the woofs out of that cow's back, I went over her from one end to the other and kept searching around 'til I found out she also had the hollow-tail.

"And the judge wanted to know right there in the courtroom with me on the witness stand what was the cure, and I told him. He didn't interrupt me then, neither. All you do is lay the soft piece of the tail on a little wooden block and take a real sharp knife and cut plumb down the length of the hollow spot from top to bottom. You lay that hollow wide open and you pack it full of a mixture of table salt and black pepper, and then you tie it up with a rag real tight for ten days or two weeks and they get well.

"And the judge said, 'Did you treat the animal under question in such a fashion, Miz Simpson?'

"I said, 'Yes, sir, judge, your honor, I did.'

"And he asked me, 'And then what happened?'

"I rared back and looked him in the eye and said, 'Judge, your honor, sir, I ain't seen her since.'

"Well, sir, it like to broke up meeting. Everybody laughed so hard the judge had to bang for quiet. He was a great one for truth and facts, that judge was, and all he done after that was ask the Watkins man if to his knowledge there was such a disease as hollow-tail. Of course, the Watkins man had to say there was or look like a fool in front of the whole county. I mean, folks can forgive a judge for not knowing no better, but that Watkins man didn't have no excuse. Soon as he said, 'Yes, sir,' that judge slammed down his whatyoumaycallit real loud and said, 'I find in favor of the defendant. Case closed. Court dismissed!' And that, as they say, was all she wrote."

Whenever we see a painting of a dirt road that meanders between a man's barn and his dwelling house, we tend to be reminded of a quieter, more peaceful time.

That may be an error in perception.

JIM HARRISON

RED
GOOSE
SHOES
RED
GOOSE
SHOES
ALL LEATHER FOR
BOYS AND GIRLS
JIM HARRISON

DRINK
JIM HARRISON

A LITTLE FULL

*B*EFORE I was born we had saloons in Georgia. My granddaddy told me. After I was born we had Prohibition. My daddy told me. Each of them was an expert, and they knew what they were talking about.

My granddaddy said that every little settlement of any note used to have a wooden building where a man could buy a drink of red liquor and visit with neighbors over the course of a rainy afternoon that precluded farming. Sometimes it was a long rainy spell, and sometimes a man got carried away in conviviality, and sometimes a man just plain had a hankering for it. Not infrequently a citizen would get a dram or two too many, a condition my granddaddy referred to as being "a little full."

He loved to tell about the night his nephew came home when he was more than a little full. He never referred to that nephew by just his first name, but always as "Will Sams." Will Sams had married a Hodnett, a fact that gave a man forever a certain stature and luster of respectability in our community that could be diminished but never erased by misdeeds on his part. The Hodnett girls were ladies, they had been raised right, they were the supreme example of "Blood will tell," and blood was what counted in Fayette County because the environment was the same for everyone and didn't amount to much.

"Will Sams came home well after dark one night; his wife and children were already in bed. Mamie (she was a Hodnett) heard him bumping up the steps and falling against the doorjamb and got up to let him in.

"Will Sams evidently had got hold of some bad liquor that evening, and more than likely had more than a bait of it, for he was pretty full. Will Sams was bad to drink every now and then. He just fell in the door that night and grabbed his wife.

"'Mamie, I'm sick.'

"Mamie (she was a saint as well as a Hodnett) said, 'Yes, darling, I know you're sick.' And Will Sams begged, 'Help me, Mamie.'

"Mamie was leading him to the bed fast as she could, with him as limber-legged as he was, and she said, 'Yes, darling, I'm helping you.' She got him to the bed and laid out on it, and Will Sams said, 'Mamie, I tell you I'm sick. I mean, I'm sick enough to die. Mamie, I want you to pray for me.'

"And Mamie was pulling off his shoes and socks and she said, 'Of course, darling, I'll pray for you.'

"And Will Sams hollered, 'Mamie, I mean it when I say I want you to pray for me. I really think I'm dying. I want you to pray for me now. Quit messing around with them shoes and socks, and pray for me right now, this very minute. Before it's too late.'

"And that sweet, patient Mamie did as she was told. She knelt down by the side of the bed, folded her hands, bowed her head and said, 'Dear Lord, look down in thy infinite love and mercy and take pity on my poor drunken husband.'

"And Will Sams raised his head up off of the pillow and hollered, 'Hell, Mamie! Don't tell Him I'm drunk!'"

My granddaddy used to tell that story, slapping his thigh and laughing until the tears came.

Mr. Israel Emmanuel Lindler was a respected citizen in the community, renowned for siring five daughters who were the loveliest young ladies in the panhandle of Clayton County, all of them except Lilla being taller than their father. He was the son of Dutch immigrants who had somehow stumbled on the secret that there was a civilization south of New York state. Mr. Israel had acquired a cotton plantation with all the trimmings, such as a sackful or two of twenty-dollar gold pieces and a slave or so. The War got the trimmings, but Mr. Lindler held onto the land. He also retained his dignity. He settled into the lifestyle of Reconstruction gentry in our area, impecunious but proud, not above manual labor in the fields, rearing his daughters to be ladies and hold their heads up. They were a credit to him and were referred to, far and wide, as those "good-looking Lindler girls."

One dreary afternoon, Mr. Lindler saddled his mule, having long since sold the horses and stored the carriage but having managed to hang onto his fine leather saddle. He rode into Lovejoy Station and tied the mule to a post at the saloon. Many friends came in and out that afternoon, and Mr. Lindler lingered until nearly all of them left. When he departed, there was no doubt that he was a little full, for he put his left foot into the stirrup on the right side of the mule and swung himself astride the patient animal. There he sat in silver-haired aplomb with imperturbable dignity, erect as Buddha, and clucked to the mule still tied to the post.

A fledgling teenager, clear-eyed and realistic, spoke cheerfully and respectfully. "Mr. Israel, how come you sitting up there on that old mule backwards?"

Mr. Lindler considered him long enough to focus his eyes and become aware of his own spatial position. If he felt challenged or defensive, he masked it well. He roared at the youth, "Young man, how in the hell do you know which way I'm going?"

My father used to tell that story, slapping his thigh and laughing until the tears came. Then he'd wipe his eyes, and once he said to me, "Most of us spend more time looking where we've been than where we are headed, and there are a considerable number of people who are sitting in the saddle backwards."

No saloon was painted with Coca-Cola signs in the days of Mr. Israel Lindler or of Will Sams. Coca-Cola came later, and its advertising push much later. My grandmother said that when it first came out the drink had real cocaine in the formula, just a little bit. She said that's how it got its name, and that's also why everybody referred to a bottle of it as a "dope." My grandmother had more opinions than facts, but she acted firmly on both. As long as she was mistress of her own home, Coca-Cola and whiskey were banned from it. My grandfather kept his whiskey in the corncrib and went up the road to Mr. Ed Hightower's store when he wanted a Coca-Cola. He spent more time in the corncrib than he did in Hightower's store.

When on rare occasions I get myself invited to an event at the Piedmont Driving Club, I revel in the opulence there. I survey the tasteful furnishings, the sparkling chandeliers and, relishing the contrast in my surroundings, I recall the dingy saloon at Lovejoy.

I observe the refinement of mixed drinks and cocktails served in delicate crystal, the mannerly elegance with which modern ladies and gentlemen sip therefrom, and I remember the men of my South, the stalwarts of frontier Georgia who drank their liquor red or white, but drank it straight and drank it raw. I see some people in the city groups today who can still be identified as being a little full.

I remember Will Sams. Pray for me now, Mamie, and don't tell Him I'm drunk.

Most of all, though, I look around, and I remember Mr. Israel Lindler. I cannot help wondering, "How in the hell do we know which way we're going?"

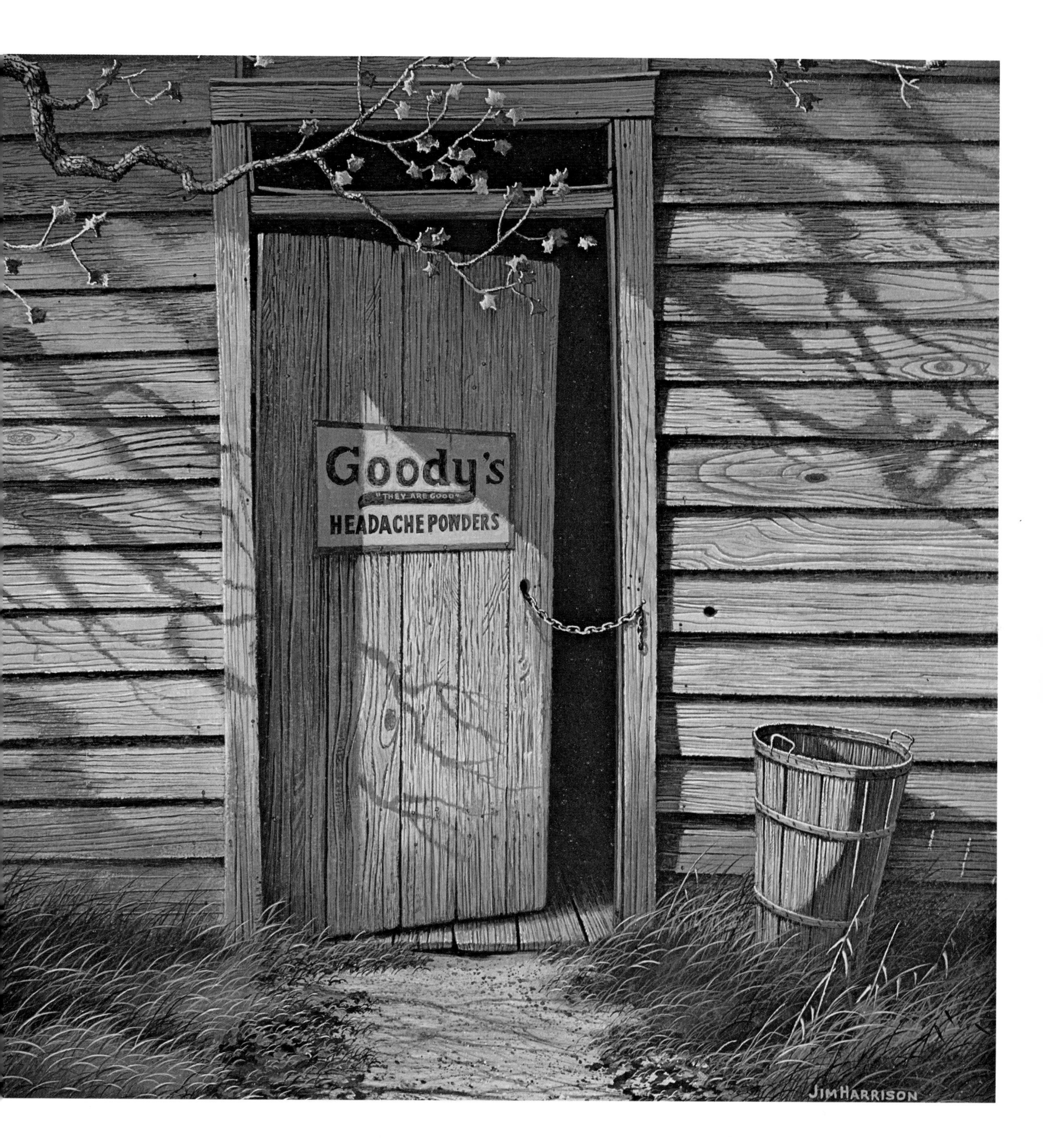
Goody's
"THEY ARE GOOD"
HEADACHE POWDERS
JIM HARRISON

JIM HARRISON

THE BUCKET

A BUCKET serves many purposes, and the sight of one carries a man back. One that did not leak was a treasure and was not to be used carelessly for potatoes or corn or cow feed or wood ashes or to strew guano or such. An old banged-up bucket with a little daylight showing through served well enough for those chores. A good bucket, one with its bottom still intact, was kept clean and used for liquids. About every two hours in April and May and even oftener when the sun really got hot in June and July, a child too young for heavy work drew water up from the deep well beneath the white oak tree and carried a bucketful around the fields. Sometimes there was a gourd dipper, sometimes one of tin, and sometimes just an old fruit jar from which to drink. The plowman and the hoe hands didn't care about that. The water was always clear and so fresh that it raised a cold sweat on the outside of the bucket by the time it got to the field, and the workers were grateful. The sweat they had raised was not a cold one.

Izee had a bucket of her own, but she did not carry water to the field hands in it. She was not that dependable. Sometimes she went along the terraces or the edges of the woods and filled her bucket with dewberries or the sensual clusters of wild strawberries. Like as not, she might eat them all herself before she got home with them. Izee was her own person and kept to herself. She wouldn't speak to white folks, not a single word. She went her own way, too, and would wander up unexpectedly at almost anyplace on the farm. She stayed with Aunt Boo who was her grandmother and was said to have some Indian blood in her. Her mother was Classie Mae. My grandfather said that Classie Mae was a "high yellow." My mother said that Classie Mae was a "high stepper." Whatever she was remained a mystery to me.

When Izee was six months old, Classie Mae threw down her hoe handle and walked out of the cotton field one day and left. Everybody thought she had just stepped out until they got home that night. New York, New York, was where she ended up, but she started out in Detroit, they said. Every few years she would come home to see Aunt Boo. She always arrived with a different man, and my grandfather said every time she came she was a shade lighter. My mother's lips would get thin, but she didn't say anything. When my mother did not approve of someone, she did not have to tell you. You could look at her and tell for yourself. I liked to look at Classie Mae. She used heavy stuff on her eyelashes, had a gold tooth in front and wore real high heels with straps around the ankles.

Aunt Boo had thick white braids, no teeth at all, went barefoot and wore a Liberty-head dime on a greasy string around one ankle. You couldn't look at her and tell that she was any kin at all to Classie Mae. You couldn't look at Izee and tell she was kin to either of them.

Izee was so black that my grandfather said you couldn't even see her in the back of a cow stall. She had the biggest, thickest scars on her face that I ever saw and the most of them. They came from her having fits and falling down and getting cut. Aunt Boo called them "spells." One of Izee's arms was slicked over all the way up to her neck and jaw with running scars as patterned as a sand bed in the field after a heavy rain. That had been caused from her falling in the fire with a spell when she was three. They said that she chewed her tongue and jerked all over, too, but spells were very private things, I thought, and I never witnessed one.

Izee understood what everybody said to her, for her eyes would glitter and she would grind her teeth. She made my mother nervous. My mother insisted on calling her "Isaiah." She thought colored people had idiosyncrasies of pronunciation and that they must have given her a Bible name. It didn't make any sense at all to name a child something that had never been heard before. My mother was a very reasoned and orderly person. Aunt Boo and Classie Mae forgave her those idiosyncrasies and called their oddling "Izee."

Aunt Boo's cow went dry one time, and my mother told her that we would be glad to share. Izee came every morning with her bucket and waited till the churning was done. My mother would fill her bucket with buttermilk and about once a week would also send Aunt Boo a pound of butter. She would give Izee detailed instructions about getting the milk and butter home while they were fresh. She persisted every time in calling her "Isaiah" and asking her a direct question. Always Izee turned away in total silence with glittering eyes, and every time my mother's lips would thin.

One of my jobs was to gather the eggs, and I had been scolded because my yield was small. At least three of the hens must have stolen nests, I was told, and I was admonished to search the barn and outbuildings carefully. One beautiful May morning, I came out from behind a crepe myrtle bush after a fruitless foray to discover Izee sidling down one side of the henhouse after her visit to my mother's kitchen. One, two, three, four nests she visited to retrieve a freshly laid egg from each and drop it carefully into her bucket of concealing buttermilk. My consternation at the deed was compounded by horror at the unwashed condition of some of the eggs.

"Izee!" I called. "That's stealing."

She showed no startle in response, but turned slowly in her sack-like shift of a tattered dress that was no particular color at all and looked at me. Her eyes glittered like black patent-leather buttons. For the only time in my life, Izee spoke to me.

"I ain't studying you, white boy," she said.

Buckets serve many purposes. Just looking at one can make a man remember.

FRESH
GRITS
JIM HARRISON

SEE
ROCK CITY
WORLD'S EIGHTH WONDER
JIM HARRISON

FAIRBANK'S
GOLD
DUST
WASHING POWDER
JIM HARRISON

JIM HARRISON

SNOWY MEMORY

IT HARDLY ever snowed enough to stick when I was growing up. Whenever it did, there was jubilation in the land. Children could not get to school, and grown folks who went to public work stayed home, too. There was none of their regular work that farmers could do, and everyone in the countryside relaxed into an unexpected holiday. It was a family time.

Mothers made snow cream with milk, sugar and vanilla, so cold it made a hurting in your chest if you swallowed too fast, and your eyeballs ached if you held it in your mouth and tried to swallow slowly. Fathers, who were customarily obsessed with the serious business of earning a living, cast off their dignity like Sunday suits to make snowmen and otherwise cavort in the snow with their children. When snow was on the ground, laughter rang like bells into the sky.

Everything looked wonderfully different when buried in snow. The dirty and the ugly were immediately covered, the universe looked clean. Reflected light from snow-covered earth gave human faces a luminosity, an unaccustomed radiance. In the new fallen softness, it was possible to follow the hieroglyphs left by rabbit feet to the secret burrows beneath the white hummock of a broomsedge clump or the rounded hillock of a brush pile. Snow was magic.

Everett Greer was a dapper little martinet of a man, neat of feature, impeccable in dress, proud of person. He was the only man in Fayetteville who could have his nails manicured or wear a cashmere coat and not be labeled a sissy. He had been born and raised in north Georgia and said they always thought up there that a snowfall was might nigh good as the Second Coming. The only thing about him bigger than his temper was his heart.

Back in '39, there came the best snowstorm anybody could remember, and Everett threw a yelling, stomping, purple-faced fit right in the middle of it. Those that were privileged to witness both storm and fit were never able later on to decide which had been the more impressive natural phenomenon.

The snow came through in the daytime. It came down without any wind in it at all, so thick it ran everything in town off the streets. A bunch of folks congregated in Seawright's Drugstore, the excitement of the unexpected making everybody talk louder and laugh harder than they normally would. They said everything they could think of about the snow, drank their quota of Coca-Colas, then began playing pool while they waited for the snow to let up so they could get home.

Not Everett. He stood in the door and watched the weather. The red mud road around the square was covered in no time. The snow came down faster and faster and got thicker and thicker on the ground. The man was bemused by the tranquillity of the experience. The whole world was white; the whole world was clean; Fayetteville was quieter than it had ever been before. The snowflakes were big and feathery, and the only sound that Everett could hear was the kiss and whisper of those flakes as they brushed each other in their fall from the sky. They came down so thick that he could barely make out the outline of the old courthouse across the street, and when the booming and reverberating clock struck three, the sound was flat and distant, muted by the snow. Everett said later that he hadn't felt that peaceful since he moved to Fayetteville.

Standing in the open doorway, lost in wonder, oblivious to the pool game in the back of the store, he became aware presently that someone had moved across the doorway from him. Looking across, he saw that it was James Marvin Hill.

Everett, as noted, had been raised elsewhere. All he knew

about James Marvin Hill was that he was approximately thirteen or fourteen years old, that his mother had died when he was five, and that the reserved and overly proper Mr. Marvin Hill had raised James Marvin and his younger brother the best he could without ever marrying again.

Everett was aware that James Marvin's mother had been a McEwing, and he was certainly aware of the harum-scarum reputation all the McEwings enjoyed in our town. He saw now only an adolescent, wistful-looking demi-orphan leaning against the doorjamb across from him, looking into the thickly falling snowflakes. Everett's heart was touched.

"Isn't it beautiful, son?"

James Marvin looked solemnly into the snow and replied, "Yes, sir, it is. You know, Mr. Greer, every time it snows it makes me think of my momma."

Everett's heart expanded. "Does it, son?"

"Yes, sir. We was living in that little house Mr. Dan Stevens owns now. Brother William was just a baby and was in the middle of the floor playing with his blocks. Momma was on one side of the fireplace darning socks, and Poppa was on the other studying some papers he had brought home. I'll never forget it. All of a sudden, Momma flung her darning gourd clean across the room and hit Poppa up side the head with it and yelled, 'For God's sake, Marvin, say something! It's quiet as a cat pissing in a snowbank!'"

Everett drew himself up, pointed an imperative finger and shouted, "Get yourself back to that pool table where you belong, you insensitive young whippersnapper!"

Then he jumped up and down, turned purple and said it again.

Of such stuff are memories made. Ever since Everett Greer told me that story, I think of him whenever it snows.

NCLE JOHN'S
SYRUP
JIM HARRISON

JIM HARRISON

0322
ATLANTIC COAST LINE
JIM HARRISON

CABOOSE

IN MY childhood, there was a song, now imperfectly recalled from the dim and distant layers of a merciful memory. I was no more gifted at singing than I was at playing baseball, but I learned early on that there are times in life when it is preferable to endure any group activity than to suffer exclusion and loneliness. Therefore, I shrieked along, tone deaf and tuneless, in a never-identified key, comforting myself the while with the assurance that at least I knew the words. Now they are gone. The refrain, however, was "Little red caboose, little red caboose, little red caboose behind the train."

The railroad tracks were two miles distant from our farm but ran no more than thirty yards behind Joe-Joe's house. On the afternoons when my mother visited Miss Annie, I was allowed to go along and play, a rare opportunity for association with my white peers that my mother felt should be encouraged. I have never forgotten the freight trains that traversed the railroad cut behind that home.

Joe-Joe taught me that you could put an ear to the rails Indian fashion and tell that a train was coming from miles away. Crossed nails placed on the track would be flattened and molded together in the semblance of little scissors, and a copper penny would be squeezed into an elongated oval that was a great curiosity, although it immediately lost its buying power.

The most fun about the train, however, was its passage. The mere presence of such an unlikely and transient eruption in the bucolic serenity of a lazy afternoon was an excitement. First there was the tremor. Before the ear picked up any sound, there was shaking of the earth, a low-pitched, inundating vibration coming up from bedrock and topsoil through the feet and into the vitals, melding place, person and event in a thrilled unit of time. Next came the barely audible rumble and rhythmic chugging of the great black engine, followed rapidly by the arrogant whistle, two longs and a short, to fling warning across the countryside that this was no ordinary train, that it would not stop at the depot or even slow for the crossing at Woolsey. Let wagons and automobiles beware, this freight was coming through.

Standing bravely in the face of fear on the shoulder in the cut behind Joe-Joe's house, I can remember the engine's passing. The earth beneath my feet vibrated so vigorously with the weight and motion that my vision shimmered in temporary dance. I could hear the deep belching sough of the steam in the engine chambers, feel the heat from the firebox, see the well-oiled robot arms moving rhythmically in glistening push and pull to turn the mighty wheels. Then the coal smoke would fill the air in the cut, thicker and stronger than the flatulence from two thousand cornfed mules, a repugnant but fascinating experience that was mercifully brief. Then the engine was gone.

The freight cars followed along with rattle and clatter and click, the music of their passing changed in pitch by the weight within individual cars, the jostling of their couplings an unexpected tambourine. They seemed an interminable chain, but finally came the caboose. Improbable little wooden house on wheels, always painted red, always a story and a half with a protruding stovepipe, always reminiscent of Toonerville Trolley in the funny papers, it trundled along at the tail of the train like the last child on a pop-the-whip line. I loved the caboose.

I would leap to a crosstie between the rails to wave and wave as it pulled away from me and out of my life forever. The first caboose I ever saw was occupied by a man sitting upstairs, corpulent body packed into overalls made of blue-and-white striped cloth like the ticking from my grandmother's feather bed, a visored cap of the same material squarely atop his head. Plainly across the bib of the overalls, I could see the loop of a watch chain shining gold. As I waved in a frenzy at the caboose, the engine, the entire train, the placid man removed the toothpick from his mouth in casual salute but never stirred his massive torso. Right then, I wanted worse than anything to ride in a caboose, to be pulled days on end through unfolding countryside with no effort at all on my part.

I shared that dream when I was nearly grown. I was digging holes and stringing fence with Son John Jones, burdened forever with the sobriquet bestowed at his mother's knee—by his mother. Son John had a right eye that roamed sightlessly all over the place when he engaged in conversation. He could be persuaded to do work for day wages when he was caught up with his own crop, but he let it be known that it was a favor and he was not obliged to do it. He stopped whenever it suited him to roll and lick and smoke a cigarette. He probably had an ancestor at Hastings, no more literate than he but every bit as determined.

While he was crimping the end of a fresh Prince Albert cigarette, striking a match on the fastener of his overalls, and while I waited with hammer and staples to resume stringing the sharp-tufted barbed wire taut enough to sing, the four o'clock freight blew for the crossing at Woolsey. Coming across the fields and woods and swamps, the whistle sounded far away and lonesome, haunting, calling.

"Son John," I said, "all my life, I've wanted to ride in the caboose on the tail end of a long freight train and not even know where the train was going."

The eye rolled rapidly like a bleached blue marble. I tried to concentrate on the steady one.

"I use to feel like you do about a caboose, but let me tell you what happened. I recollect talking to old man I. E. Collier once when I was about your age and size and telling him about wanting to ride a caboose. Old man I.E. remembered when the railroad tracks was first laid, out yonder across Rareover and

Shakerag districts. Said the railroad company didn't pay nothing much at all for the right-of-way. They claimed it was gonna raise everbody's land values so much the farmers ought to pay them, but they did promise anybody who signed a free ride when the line was done and the trains commenced to running.

"Old man I.E. was just a young fellow, not old enough to grow no mustaches but old enough to smell his own pee and be studying on girls a little bit. He wasn't what you would call sparking Musetty Tinsley, but he had ast her to ast her Pa, Mr. Babe Tinsley, if it was all right if he could come set with her some evening.

"Well, it turned out the time old man I.E. went calling on Musetty was on the evening of the day that Mr. Babe Tinsley got his free ride on the train.

"I know you don't recollect Mr. Babe at all, for he died before you was born, but let me tell you, he was as plain-spoken a man as you could find in the whole county, independent as a hog on ice. When he was signing up for the tracks to go across the back of his fifty acres, he was like you a-talkin now. Nothing would do him but he'd get to ride in the caboose when it come his turn to go, although everbody else had rode up front on a passenger train.

"Old man I.E. had been setting up with Musetty in the front room that evening 'til well after dark. Said it was getting on late enough he thought Miz Tinsley was fixin to tell him it was time to go. Mr. Babe had been gone since first light and hadn't carried nothing but a little ole sack lunch with him to eat cause the train was only going fifty miles down the road to La Grange. His womenfolks was commencing to worry a little cause it was getting late.

"Well, sir, the door flew open, and there he was. Old man I.E. said Mr. Babe had on stiff new overalls and had wore his jumper with a white shirt buttoned up all the way at the neck. He was dressed up like a sore thumb. Never said a word, Mr. Babe didn't, not even "Hidy" to old man I.E., just went over and set hisself down on one corner of the bed with his hands hanging down between his legs.

"Miz Tinsley jumped out of her rocking chair and run outside to the spring house and brought Mr. Babe a big ole glass of buttermilk, and he dreened it without ever letting it down. Then he wiped his mouth with the back of his hand and let out a long sigh, a big belch, and said, 'Aye, Lord.'

"With that he pulled off his shoes and dropped them and then commenced to jooging between his toes with a sock, like you'll do when its been a long, hot day and you got all that ole stuff, you know, between your toes. He never noticed old man I.E. yet, just sat there on the bed, jooging and a-pickin.

"Old man I.E. said it kinda got off with him, and he could tell Musetty was what you might call a little mortified 'cause she squirmed around a bit and said, 'How was it, Pa?'

"Mr. Babe put his heel down on the floor that wasn't made out of nothin but puncheons, flung his sock across the room and said, 'I ain't got no idea how big this world really is, but you young folks can mark down one thing for sure and certain. If it stretches as far thataway,' and he pointed east, 'as it does thataway' and he pointed west toward La Grange, 'I'm here to tell you it's a golly whopper!"

"Old man I.E. said he never went back to see Musetty. Said ever time he saw her he could smell Mr. Babe's sock sailing across the room and see them white, shriveled toes shining in the lamplight. She went on and married old man Eli Banks, Musetty did, and had nine to ten chappies—I don't recollect which.

"Old man I.E. and I, neither one, wasn't what nobody would call delicate, but ever since he told me about settin up with Musetty, I ain't had no desire at all to ride on no little red caboose behind no train."

JIM HARRISON

HERSHEY'S
MILK CHOCOLATE
ALMONDS 5¢

CLABBER GIRL The Healthy
BAKING POWDER
JIM HARRISON

MEN OF WORTH

A REALLY solid town, one destined to outlast the folk who settled it and to endure through the decline or even the disappearance of the descendants of those settlers, started off with stores that were built sturdily of brick. Wood rotted or burned; brick lasted. If those stores happened to be across the street from the courthouse, it was ordained that they would be prosperous establishments, an investment in real estate that could not be less than profitable.

Not only was Cam Bennett one of the pioneers of Fayette County in the third decade of the last century; he was also a strong businessman with an eye to the future. He built a string of stores on the west side of the courthouse square. He built every one of them with slave labor from hand-pressed bricks. He built them with decorative cornices and fretwork across the top. They stand today. The tin-roofed shelter down the length of the sidewalk is gone, the benches and hitching rack long since torn away, the watering trough at the curb destroyed, the well in the middle of the intersection filled in and paved over. The stores, however, have endured.

Mr. Cam owned considerable acreage spreading west of the courthouse, on out past Lake Bennett and up Gingercake for miles. He had a policy of deeding without fee an acre of ground to any group that wanted to build a church. He had eight children, six girls and two boys. When they married, Mr. Cam gave each of them a store on the square, five hundred acres of land

and a house he built for them on any site they chose. When he died, he still possessed thirty thousand acres of land, a passel of slaves and a good name.

Today, he has many descendants, but only a handful of them live in the county, ten of them on land that he once owned. Only one of the stores is still in the family; it belongs to a great-granddaughter who does not live here anymore. A man, no matter how smart he may be, is influenced more by what's behind him than what's in front of him; he reacts more to knowledge than he does to vision. It is a manifestation of his character when a man can utilize both. Mr. Cam Bennett was an exceptional man.

So was Abraham Rosenbloom. While the Bennett children were living through the rending upheaval of Reconstruction, selling their inheritances for bread or losing land to harsh taxes, learning that past grandeur does not guarantee present or future security, Abe Rosenbloom came among them. He did not stay in town. He rode in on the train with a pack that was as big as he and almost as heavy, for he was a diminutive man with short, bowed legs. He shouldered his pack at the depot and began walking. He walked the larger dirt roads, then the smaller ones and finally the trails. He covered the county. At every house he stopped and offered his wares for sale.

He was always invited in, and the entire family gathered around while he displayed buttons, needles, ribbons, shoelaces, bolts of cloth, anything that he could pack in on his back to the isolated rural areas and sell. Wherever he was at mealtime, he was invited to eat; wherever he was when darkness descended, he was invited to spend the night. The South was ever a hospitable area, and Mr. Rosenbloom was an adaptable man.

Miss Mae Harp is nearly a hundred, and she remembers him well. "All us children were crazy about Mr. Rosenbloom. For that matter, Mama and Papa and Granny North thought a heap of him, too. Come to think of it, everybody all over the county liked Mr. Rosenbloom, but the children were especially glad to see him.

"We didn't get much company in those days, and it was a red-letter day when we'd spy Mr. Rosenbloom coming up the road. He always tried to time it so's he'd get to our house late enough in the evening he could spend the night with us. Papa was a welcoming man and glad to have the peddler. Mama said the poor fellow had to stay sometimes at places where the woman just wasn't any kind of housekeeper at all, and then, too, some folks were so bad off they didn't have sheets for the bed. A lot of homes didn't have anything for mattresses but those made out of corn shucks, or else bed ticks stuffed with straw.

"Mr. Rosenbloom would get in the front bedroom and spread out his pack, and when Mama and Granny North had picked what they wanted, he'd have a little present for us children. We were crazy about him.

"He was different from us; he was a Jew. Come from Russia or Germany or some such place as that. But he'd always set up to the table while Papa asked the blessing in Christ's name and all, and he ate whatever we ate. Except he wouldn't eat pork. No, he absolutely would not eat pork. If we happened to have meat when he was there, he'd always ask what it was, and he just wouldn't touch hog meat. Course, a heap of the time all we'd have would be a big pot of greens, 'cause times were hard back then and we ate what we had and what we could get. Mr. Rosenbloom could put away as much cornbread and buttermilk and turnip salad as most men twice his size. Granny North said wasn't any use telling him what the greens were seasoned with. We never did, and if they hurt him, you couldn't tell it.

"He sure never quit being a Jew. I used to wonder where he'd come from across the ocean where things could have been so bad for him that he thought he was better off walking the roads of Fayette County, winter and summer, hot or cold, uphill and downhill, rain or shine, with that heavy old pack on his back. He never complained. He saved his money, and after a few years, first news you know, he bought a horse and buggy and could carry a heap more goods with him. Then it seemed like no time at all, he'd bought that corner store in town from one of Mr. Cam Bennett's boys, I think it was the one what left and moved to Douglasville, but I'm not sure.

"Anyhow, there he stayed till he died. 'Rosenbloom's Mercantile. Dry Goods and Notions.' Here come his wife into town, and we didn't even know he had one. She was shorter and more duck-legged than he was, and it was harder to catch everything she said when she talked. They lived back of Doctor Wallis, in that house Louie Graves owns now, and kept pretty much to themselves. I always liked Mrs. Rosenbloom myself. She did finally join the Eastern Star, and it was funny when she'd get outdone with him and they'd start jabbering at each other in some kind of foreign tongue. We'd sit around and listen and couldn't understand a word they said.

"But they did well. Mr. Rosenbloom had been so nice to farm folks that when they found he'd opened a store in town, they just naturally traded with him. You could always count on him for a donation if a church anywhere in the county needed pews or a new roof or some such. He stayed a Jew till he died though. Used to take his chickens or geese or ducks on the train up to Atlanta every Friday morning alive and bring them back dead on the first train after dinner. Took them up there to have the rabbi kill them for him in some sort of special way. 'Rabbi' is what they called their preacher, and they counted on him to do all sorts of strange things for them. I remember Mr. Rosenbloom well."

So do my sister and I. To this day. Jimmie Kate remembers going in his store with our mother and his giving her a small pocketbook when she was still a young child. He put five pennies in the new purse and said, "Now you haf someting you can carry to Sunday School and you haf also someting you can put in the collection plate."

I remember his bringing twelve young ducks to me when I was ten. The trade was that I would feed them for four months and then he would come back to get them and pay me twenty-five cents per duck. I was to furnish the corn. Since our crib was packed with a bumper crop, I regarded this as manna from Heaven. "Vun of dem," he cautioned me, "is a runt. Perhaps you should be feeding him a little extra."

He was right. The other ducks grew so fast that you could tell it daily, but they would lower their outstretched necks to the ground, scissor their bills threateningly and chase the runt away from the feed. He had to fight and steal for every grain of corn he got, and he did not thrive. One day I captured him and put him in a box with dried butterbeans my mother had garnered for seed and watched with pity as he gorged himself. I can still hear the dry clattering sounds as he gulped until he could swallow no more. I remember my feeling of virtue as I watched him waddle to the watering trough, his hunger for once abated. I remember the horror when I found him the next morning. He was cold and stiff, his stomach split wide open, swelled butterbeans spilling from his craw. I remember the guilt when I looked Mr. Rosenbloom in the eye on his return to gather the ducks.

"The runt died," I said, with no explanation.

"No matter," he replied. "Ve all do. You fed dem vell, dey are nice fat ducks." And he insisted on paying me my quarter for the runt. Jimmie Kate and I have liked Jews ever since. We remember Mr. Rosenbloom well.

Barney Ballew was not a man to own a store himself like Mr. Cam Bennett and Mr. Rosenbloom did. He had no ambition in that direction. Instead, he hung out in stores and made witty, caustic remarks about passers-by. His favorite store was John M. Jackson and Sons, an emporium across town near the depot. Kate Greer was a generation later than Miss Mae Harp and died a generation earlier. She is the one who told me about the time Barney put the whole town in an uproar.

"We had a doctor here back then named Dr. Grizzard, like in 'buzzard' and 'gizzard.' I guess he was a pretty good doctor, but Mama always called Dr. Lester to us, except she'd use Dr. Wallis if she thought it might be pneumonia. Dr. Grizzard lived right across the railroad tracks in the house where Mae Harp moved to look after Hoss and Russ when they left the farm. He had a little office in the back yard and everything.

"They didn't have any children, and Mrs. Grizzard was bad to put on airs, which didn't make her the most popular woman in town by any means, although she wanted to be. She had a little poodle dog that she acted a stomp-down fool over, and everybody sort of sniggered behind her back and overlooked her. One afternoon she gave that poodle a bath and fluffed and combed him to a fare-thee-well, and then, so help me Hannah, she tied a big pink bow ribbon around his neck with a card that said, 'I am Mrs. Grizzard's little dog. Whose little dog are you?'

"Then she pushed him out the door and let him cross the railroad tracks and head up the sidewalk. First thing you know, he went prissing and trembling into John M. Jackson and Sons with that ribbon around his neck, just as full of himself as Jack David Phillips ever was when he was a little boy and dressed up for Sunday School. Barney Ballew was there with three or four of his cronies, and in no time at all, that little poodle came tearing down the street, 'Yip, yip, yip!' past Kitchens Store ninety to nothing.

"The harder he ran, the louder he yipped. His little fluffy ears were strung straight out behind him, and he jumped the railroad tracks, Jim Kitchens said, without touching a crosstie. Mrs. Grizzard heard him coming and ran out on the front porch, and the little beastie jumped in her arms still yelling like a banshee.

"Somebody had put another card on the ribbon, and this one said, 'I've got turpentine on my little asshole. What have you got on yours?'

"Well, sir, all hell broke loose on Railroad Street. Mrs. Grizzard went into hysterics! She cranked up the operator and screamed for her to ring every phone in town till she found Doctor Grizzard and to send him home, that she had an emergency. Doctor Grizzard got home and got some lard on little Poochie-Pie, and then he got out his pistol and went to town. Jim Kitchens said that was the longest pistol she ever saw in her life. Doctor Grizzard paced up and down the middle of the big road, waving it around and yelling for the craven coward who had done such a thing to step out and own up to it. Jim said he drew a pretty big crowd, but it was the quietest one she'd ever seen. Said Barney Ballew leaned against the doorjamb at John M. Jackson and Sons cleaning his fingernails with his pocket knife and, for once in his life, never had a word to say.

"Doctor Grizzard packed up his wife and dog and moved to Atlanta. Changed his name to Griz-*zard* and had himself paged at the Loewe's Grand Theater till he got famous. He wound up with a whole raft of society patients and joined the Athletic Club. He never got himself into Capital City or the Piedmont Driving, but he did die rich. All on account of Barney Ballew, who we practically had to take up a collection to put away when he eventually up and died."

Mr. Cam Bennett and Mr. Abe Rosenbloom knew what was behind them, and they also had the vision to look ahead. They owned the brick stores. They were exceptional men. They have contributed to our heritage.

Barney Ballew lived only for the present. He hung out in the stores of other people. He poked fun at folks and laughed a lot. He was also exceptional. All of these men contribute to our memories.

Who's to judge?

JIM HARRISON

TUBE ROSE
SCOTCH SNUFF
JIM HARRISON

CALL IT PROGRESS

MOST THINGS in life have not erupted to fruition after careful planning, but have evolved along the path of least resistance. We may admire the concept of Pallas Athena springing full grown from the fertile brain of Zeus, but our heart is with Aphrodite, who comes to us with careless laughter from out the fragile foam of the sea.

Washington, DC, was laid out and planned before the first footing was dug. So was Brasilia. But most towns in rural America just sort of grew up around whatever was there first: a road, a train track, a general store, a pretty grove of oaks. The grouping of a brick store, a wooden side building, the residence of the merchant a little distance away, was sufficient nidus for a city in days gone by. If anyone had anticipated the marriage of internal combustion to gasoline, then someone surely would have planned for traffic. Instead, it evolved around and over us and now threatens to swallow us alive.

Before the automobile, rules of traffic were based on simple courtesy, a direct interchange between individuals. The loaded wagon took right-of-way over the empty one, a buggy with ladies in it over the man astride. In the early days of the automobile, these rules still applied. Cars waited patiently while first arrivals crept over narrow bridges or wallowed laboriously through mud holes. Passage over our roads may have been occasionally perilous, but traffic itself was not the danger that it later became.

Used to, we did not even have to have a driver's license, and age requirement consisted solely of individual acquisition of skill. My younger sister was only thirteen when she drove my mother's square black Chevrolet on an errand to the store. It was late summer, and the dog she carried with her undertook to jump out the rear window. My sister, temporarily injudicious in her priorities, abandoned the steering wheel to rescue the pet but never bothered to ease up on the accelerator. The car leaped a ditch, cut a swath through the jungle of a full-grown field of corn and traveled in a circle back across the ditch, full tilt into the center of the road. There my sister finally applied the brakes, with impeccable equanimity removed the cornstalks from the windshield and, as a well-conducted lady should, continued on her mission.

Today, at the same spot, she would have been sideswiped by a Porsche, had an accident report filled out by the police, been transported by ambulance on backboard and in cervical collar, investigated by the juvenile authorities and reprimanded by the Humane Society. Progress has come upon us.

Back in '38, Macon was a city of considerable size in Georgia, yet universal recognition and accommodation were accorded Miss Sally Boone, who trilled ebullient greetings to everyone she saw from behind her steering wheel while tootling her car from one side of the center line to another, occasionally even up on the sidewalk. The same regard was afforded Miss Kate Eastin in Fayetteville, except we did not have sidewalks and Miss Kate was not addicted to saluting acquaintances. She just went grimly where she was headed by the shortest route available. She was never accused of tootling.

My mother was a person of pluck, one of the earliest women from our community to tackle driving in Atlanta. She had an inner assurance that a combination of faith in God and the well-mannered charm of a Southern lady would protect her anywhere, open all doors and level some mountains. She carried this provincial belief with her into the impersonal, uncaring, sign-littered traffic arteries of Atlanta and emerged unscathed, albeit sometimes with flushed face and hat askew. I remember once she carried all four of her children on an exciting foray into the big city for Christmas shopping. We had explored Woolworth's and Kress's in careful selection of gifts we could afford and marveled at the luxurious, unobtainable wares in Rich's. In late afternoon, we were headed home, my mother a little confused at the maze of streets and her position in such a long line of automobiles. The traffic was so heavy that the lights at intersections had been supplemented by whistling, impatiently directing policemen, their uniforms accentuated by white gloves and tight collars. There was clotting cacophony at the intersection of Marietta and Spring streets, a mixture of auto horns, shrilling whistles and tinkling Salvation Army bells that embodied in the early dusk of a mid-winter day the excitement of Christmas to us country children. There were no less than five large signs that warned, in blaring black letters on white background at that intersection, "NO LEFT TURN."

As the light turned yellow, my mother exclaimed with a note of glee, "If I can just turn here on Spring Street, we'll be out of this mess in no time and make it home before dark."

My second sister opined, "But, Mother, the sign says, 'NO LEFT—.'"

"Hush, darling," she was interrupted absently, "you will make your mother nervous."

As she made her turn, the policeman gave a loud blast and an even louder bellow. "Lady! You can't do that!"

My mother leaned her head out the window a little, beamed sweetly at him, waved one hand herself in feminine direction and assured him, "Oh, yes, I can, Officer. If you'll step back just a teensy bit, I think I can squeeze through with no trouble at all."

Cars were accumulating at an unbelievable rate. The policeman assessed the practicality of his situation and reluctantly did as he was bade.

My mother rewarded him with a truly radiant smile. "Thank you, Officer. We live in Fayetteville, and my husband has a fit if I'm not home by dark."

I was only twelve, but I thought the policeman on the verge of having a fit himself. Through the rear window, I saw him resume vigorous hand signals and heard the scream of his whistle, but he was wagging his head with equal vigor in obvious disbelief.

We were decades away from traffic being that bad in our town. I remember when the only paved road in the county was the eastern end of Highway 54. The city of Fayetteville had one employee. He was a tall, genial, well-liked man of boundless good will—accommodating, cooperative and always soft-spoken. He wore the visored cap and badge of Marshall, read the water meters and drove the garbage truck. That truck was a modified pickup with wooden side bodies, and it was the only vehicle the city owned, exclusive of the fire wagon, which rested with sluggish battery in Redwine's Ford Place.

One day the marshall stopped a lady from Atlanta driving a pink Cadillac. They were at a dirt intersection two blocks from the courthouse. He tipped his hat politely and informed her that she had been speeding. She stared in disbelief and proclaimed, "I've been stopped for speeding in at least five states and ten cities, but I want you to know this is the first time in my life I've ever been given a ticket by a toothless son-of-a-bitch who hadn't shaved and was driving a goddam garbage truck!"

Our marshall immediately reduced her traffic charge to a warning, but he was transformed. At the next City Council meeting, he pounded the table with his fist and actually roared. His dictum was that he would never, ever again, stop anybody from out of town for any offense whatsoever, unless the city got him something else to drive. Shortly thereafter we bought a car with siren, flashing lights and appropriate lettering. The modern day Police Department had germinated in Fayetteville, Georgia. Progress indeed was upon us now.

Cars proliferated like living things that had no natural enemies. Children grew up through new and modern puberty rites, with the acquisition of an automobile heading the list. New residents chose our county, and each one had an automobile.

Mrs. Marc Howell was walking back across the highway from a visit to Miss Estelle Stephens one afternoon, stumbled and sprawled in abandoned disarray across the center line, well into both lanes of traffic. Because of age and infirmity, she could not get up, and no one of her grandchildren or children was quite sure how long she lay there. Each of them, however, called the doctor to come and check Mama. When I arrived, she had been enthroned in a living room chair among relatives numerous enough for Christmas dinner, her shawl in place, and only a couple of abrasions and a torn stocking as any evidence of her mishap. Soothingly, I raised my voice to accommodate her hearing loss, for she had been a Banks.

"Mrs. Howell, I think it's wonderful that you didn't break a hip or cut yourself."

She fixed her pale blue eyes on me and spoke in tones of triumph.

"Yes! And everybody was so nice to drive around me, too."

I realized that Mama Howell had witnessed a lot more of what we were calling progress than I had.

Soon we had a traffic light. Then another. And another. As traffic increased, we responded by adding more lights. The flow, but not the volume, of traffic slowed. Then someone persuaded the city fathers that the answer was to speed up the flow. We took down many of the lights and called that progress. One of our sweet ladies in desperation shut her eyes, gripped her steering wheel, and plunged into line on Highway 85. The officer investigating the wreck asked her, "Miss Mary, why did you just pull out like that when you didn't have the right-of-way?"

She looked at him piteously a moment, then squared her shoulders and tightened her lips. She had been born here; so had her parents and grandparents. With staunch sense of person and place she answered, "I had waited long enough."

So has traffic; so has progress. It builds and builds, accumulating upon itself behind the weak dam of planned growth. Then it bursts its bonds and floods the streets. Hundred-year-old trees are swept away. Antebellum and Victorian houses are bulldozed and torched. The stench of progress is in the air. It smells of raw clay and burning heart pine.

The town was born around a crossroad, a court house, a few stores. Then it just sort of grew up leisurely over the course of a careless century. It has disappeared now in the confusion of progress, the glitter of prosperity. The people mourn. The women weep.

The town is gone. We have followed the path of least resistance. That path has been broadened by, and paved with, the avarice of developers, the greed of politicians. Weep, women, weep.

JIM HARRISON

JIM HARRISON

Burma-Shave
JIM HARRISON

Calume
BAKIN
POWDE

MORTON
SALT
WHEN IT RAINS IT POURS
JIM HARRISON

Jefferson
Island
SALT
JIM HARRISON

THE PAINTINGS

Ferrol Sams, Jr., is the author of three best-selling books, *Run with the Horsemen, Whisper of the River,* and *The Widow's Mite and Other Stories.* In each of these works, he evokes the essence of small-town American life and draws his readers into that world that is fast disappearing.

A graduate of Mercer University and the Emory University School of Medicine, Sams is a practicing physician and Medical Director of the Fayette Medical Clinic.

He and his wife, Helen Fletcher, live in Fayetteville, Georgia. They have four children and ten grandchildren.

As a teenager, Jim Harrison spent his summers working with an elderly sign painter, traveling South Carolina's Low Country and painting advertisements on the sides of general stores and barns.

After majoring in education and fine art at the University of South Carolina, he became a teacher and football coach. Twelve years later, however, the longing to paint became irresistible, and he turned down a coaching offer from Furman University in order to devote himself to his art.

Since making that decision, Harrison has become one of America's foremost representational painters. Famous for his rendering of a disappearing rural America and for his paintings of advertising signs and logos inspired by his apprenticeship under J. J. Cornforth, the sign painter, he is a Frame House Gallery artist and is represented in New York by Hammer Galleries.

His previous books are JIM HARRISON, HIS WORLD REMEMBERED and PATHWAYS TO A SOUTHERN COAST. He lives in Denmark, South Carolina, with his wife, Margaret.

PLANTERS
PEANUTS
JIM HARRISON